LIONEL ADEY

C. S. Lewis's "Great War" with Owen Barfield

𝓔𝓛𝓢

English Literary Studies
University of Victoria

1978

ENGLISH LITERARY STUDIES

Published at the University of Victoria

This book has been published with the help of a grant from the Humanities Research Council of Canada, using funds provided by the Canada Council.

ISBN 0-920604-26-9

The ELS Monograph Series is published in consultation with members of the Department by ENGLISH LITERARY STUDIES, Department of English, University of Victoria, B.C., Canada

ELS Monograph Series No. 14
© 1978 by Lionel Adey

To my wife

CONTENTS

ACKNOWLEDGMENTS

A departmental colleague, Dr David Jeffrey, advised me of the Lewis (now Wade) Collection at Wheaton College, Illinois. Short visits there were funded by the University of Victoria, and a longer one by the Canada Council, which also supported research in the Bodleian Library, Oxford. Finally, a University travel grant enabled me to consult with Mr Barfield at Stony Brook College, S.U.N.Y. during his term as Visiting Professor.

To Dr Clyde Kilby, founder and Curator of the Wade Collection, and Mrs Ruth Cording, Mr Paul Snezek and Mrs McClatchey, Librarians, I am profoundly indebted for indispensable advice and assistance. In England, I received much essential information on C. S. Lewis from Rev. Walter Hooper, his assiduous secretary, editor and biographer, from the late Major W. H. Lewis, his brother, from his former colleagues and friends Mr Colin Hardie (Magdalen College, Oxford), Mr J. M. Christie, Dr R. W. Ladborough (Magdalene College, Cambridge), and also Mr Glen Cavaliero (St. Catherine's College, Cambridge) and Rev. Paris Leary (University of Leicester).

Neither this nor an earlier manuscript could have come into existence without Mr Barfield's help in supply and interpreting documents. On the previous MS much valuable advice and criticism came from my colleague Dr Patrick Grant, and from Drs George Tennyson (U.C.L.A.), Dorothy Emmet (Cavendish College, Cambridge), R. J. Reilly (University of Detroit), and Mr Harry Currie (Queen Mary College, London). On the present text, Dr George Whalley (Queen's University) has supplied many valuable suggestions and references, notably on Coleridge.

For advice and references pertaining to their fields, I am indebted to Dr Wolfe Mays (University of Manchester), and my fellow-Victorians Drs Charles Daniels and E-H. Kluge (Philosophy), Gordon Shrimpton (Classics), Michael Hadley (German) and Professors David Campbell and Herbert Huxley (Classics).

Many difficulties concerning the philosophy of Rudolf Steiner were resolved by Mr Gerald Lawrence (Rudolf Steiner Studies, Victoria), the late A. C. Harwood, friend of Lewis and Mr Barfield, and Mrs Mildred Kirkcaldy, his co-editor of the *Anthroposophical Quarterly*. Mr Barfield and Mrs

Kirkcaldy also kindly sent copies of *The Case for Anthroposophy* and *The Redemption of Thinking*, cited hereafter.

Finally two departmental colleagues, Dr Samuel Macey, General Editor of this series, and Professor Henry Summerfield, who read the proofs and supplied elusive references, have given unsparingly of their time to advise on style and format, and a third, Dr. A. S. G. Edwards, has read the galley proofs.

I can find no better words in which to thank the above-mentioned institutions and scholars than those used by Lewis, in *Surprised by Joy*, to express his gratitude to older Oxonians: "The ripest are kindest to the raw, and the most studious have the most time to spare."

LIONEL ADEY

Department of English
University of Victoria
British Columbia, Canada

PART ONE:

WHEN PHILOSOPHERS DISPUTE

CHAPTER 1

The Contestants

The dedication of C. S. Lewis's first major scholarly work, *The Allegory of Love* (1936), recalls Plato's tribute to Socrates: "To Owen Barfield, wisest and best of my unofficial teachers." This reverence does not stop Lewis from arguing brilliantly against Barfield's belief in imagination as an avenue to truth, nor from dismissing as sheer illusion Barfield's theory of a purposive "evolution of consciousness" evident in etymological change.[1] Even more explicitly Lewis rejects the idea-system of Anthroposophy that forms the keystone of Barfield's thought. Yet, while disavowing "the philosophy and theology of Dr Rudolf Steiner," Lewis describes Barfield as "the man of all my acquaintance whose character both moral and intellectual I should put highest, or very nearly so."[2] How could Lewis so venerate his "unofficial teacher" yet reject what Barfield taught?

As Lewis fully explains in his spiritual autobiography *Surprised by Joy*, Barfield delivered him from "Chronological Snobbery," the twentieth-century intellectual's inability to consider seriously ideas generated before the Enlightenment.[3] This emotional barrier cast down, Lewis could entertain belief in the supernatural, hence ultimately in Christianity, and embark on that imaginative re-creation of the medieval and renaissance worlds for which he is renowned. The scholar who would illuminate the cosmos of Chaucer and Spenser must feel at home there himself. Had Lewis remained torn between the contemptuous modern sceptic and the devourer of folk-tale and romance, he could hardly have slogged his way through so many interminable manuscripts as lie behind *The Allegory of Love* and his famous lecture-course "Prolegomena to Medieval Studies."[4] By dissolving this mental block against ideas from the past, Barfield freed Lewis to explore commentaries on old authors as "glory-holes" rather than rubbish-heaps.[5] Moreover, through arguing with Barfield, Lewis came to regard imagination as the human spirit's supreme power. It is precisely in historical imagination and empathy that he rises above any number of scholars by now better informed in matters of fact or exegesis.

In 1970, while working at Wheaton College, Illinois, amid the great collection on Lewis and associated authors amassed by Professor Clyde Kilby and now known as the Wade Collection, I came across an incomplete file of letters, all undated, together with several lengthy essays mostly set out in point form and paginated in sequence. Having once realised that these xeroxed manuscripts constituted the written remnant of the "Great War" Lewis and Barfield waged during the nineteen-twenties, I should have been wiser to extract useful information, then resume work on the critical assessment of Lewis for which the Canada Council had awarded a grant. Instead, a schoolboy urge to fill blanks and crack codes decoyed me into assigning dates, setting letters in order and inferring contents of missing items. Before long, a solemn satisfaction in being privy to weighty and mysterious arguments about *to on, poiein* and *paschein*, the One and the Many, enjoyment and contemplation, *tokos* and *dosis*—in short the secret pride in belonging to an Inner Ring, an imaginary High Table, against which Lewis so eloquently warns students—drove a bemused and distracted literary scholar to look up innumerable allusions in texts by Plato and Aristotle, to read half-forgotten modern philosophers such as Croce and Alexander, to send for out-of-print lecture-courses by Steiner and even to struggle up the foothills of Kant.

Although many a scholarly investigation has been sustained by no better motives, this one must soon have petered out but for Mr Barfield's unfailing courtesy in supplying material and explanations. As Lewis indicates, the skirmishes continued as much by word of mouth as by letter. Since Lewis rarely kept incoming letters only two are in Barfield's hand. Lewis was notoriously careless in dating his own letters, so that the only firm date in the whole set is "November, 1928" beneath his longest contribution, the two-part tractate *Clivi Hamiltonis Summae Metaphysices contra Anthroposophos* usually known as "the *Summa*" after its model by Aquinas. ("Clive Hamilton" was Lewis's early pseudonym.)

The following sequence of items and events can be pieced together from Mr Barfield's approximate dating and from information supplied in the recent biography of Lewis.[6] Late in 1921, after taking his First in English at Wadham College, Barfield began "desultory reading" for his B.Litt. thesis on "Poetic Diction." The following summer Lewis took his Double First in Literae Humaniores ("Greats") at University College, then during the 1922-23 session read Honours English, taking a First in 1923. With financial aid from his father, he spent the 1923-24 session trying to live by reviewing, but for the following session secured a *locum tenens* tutorship in Philosophy at University College and in the fall of 1925 took up an initial five-year appointment in English at Magdalen College.

Meantime Barfield had joined the anthroposophical movement founded some dozen years earlier by Rudolf Steiner following a breach with the

Theosophical Society. Barfield had been influenced to some extent by A. C. Harwood, a friend who had taken a First in Greats together with Lewis.[7]

In his journal entry dated 7 July, 1923, Lewis describes Harwood's "new philosopher," that is, Steiner, as "a sort of panpsychist, with a vein of posing superstition."[8] Lewis continues: "I was very much disappointed to hear that both Harwood and Barfield were impressed by him. The comfort they got from him (apart from the sugar plum of promised immortality . . .) seemed something I could get very much better without him."

Lewis's "Great War" with Barfield (so named after the conflict each had recently served in) arose from his efforts to dissuade Barfield from belief in Anthroposophy.

At that time Barfield had read, in English, Steiner's *Philosophy of Spiritual Activity, Occult Science* and various lecture-cycles on the Gospels. Since in a "Great War" letter Lewis mentions reading *The Way of Initiation* (now available in expanded form as *Knowledge of Higher Worlds*), Barfield presumably read that also.

In 1924-25 Barfield, recently married but able through private means to spend most of the decade as freelance scholar, began drafting his thesis. Lewis made a lengthy and detailed analysis of "Poetic Diction." The main group of "Great War" letters, written between 1925 and 1927, records his disagreement with Barfield's contention that poetry initially conveyed knowledge and that therefore imagination disseminated truth. This group of letters I call *Series I*. In a smaller group, hereafter called *Series II*, Lewis warns Barfield against submitting to spiritual direction by anthroposophical teachers. This group includes two written on Magdalen College stationery, therefore not earlier than the fall of 1925, and one enclosing a poem not written before 1929.[9]

Although Barfield did not take his degree until 1934, he had his completed thesis, including its four Appendices, accepted in 1926-27. In 1928, he published *Poetic Diction* after adding an Introduction and, by request of his publishers, the present Chapter VIII ("The Making of Meaning, II"). Lewis thought this and the preceding chapter the weakest portions. He had supplied Barfield with the frontal quotation from Aristotle's *De Anima* on active and passive reason (*poiein* and *paschein*), which Barfield re-interpreted as poetic and prosaic consciousness. Lewis also supplied "felt" in Barfield's definition of a poem's first effect, "a felt change of consciousness" in the reader. As Lewis generously insists, however, "much of that important little book" had become his by the time it was published.[10]

The same could not quite be said of Barfield's first book, *History in English Words* (1926), for although he thought well of the book Lewis disagreed with its thesis that etymological change revealed a historical evolution of consciousness. Upon the book's appearance, moreover, Lewis repeated his emphatic disagreement with a passage propounding a "great divide" throughout European philosophy between Aristotelian and Platonic traditions, and humourously threatened to "explode it in a footnote" some day.[11]

At first sight, Lewis's attack upon Anthroposophy in the *Summa* appears unconnected with his criticism of Barfield's poetic and etymological theories. What Steiner had propounded was a development from supernatural inspiration in myth and prophecy to self-enlightenment by the modern self-conscious ego. During this evolution of consciousness, imagination had played a progressively larger part in the divine education of humanity. Now, moral action should be prompted rather by an "inner lawgiver" than divine fiat.[12] For this reason, Steiner called his teaching Anthroposophy, "human wisdom," rather than Theosophy, "divine wisdom," but claimed to have discerned spiritual beings directing planetary and human evolution.

In *Poetic Diction*, Barfield distinguishes between meanings "given" in early poetry and "achieved" in the "architectonic" poetry of, for example, Vergil, as well as between primal figurative, or "poetic," and later analytical, or "prosaic," language. In *History in English Words* he traces the emergence of post-Reformation individual awareness. Though Barfield arrived at both lines of thought independently, they converge within Steiner's system.

Lewis had three reasons for wishing to dissuade Barfield from belief in the system: distrust of spirital authoritarianism, discomfort at the notion of realities conveyed by ancient myths, and unwillingness to believe that the mind could profitably observe and direct its own operations. As a pantheist, also, he found Steiner's orders of angels and demons utterly incredible.

To return to chronology, Lewis must have written his *Summa* during the summer and fall of 1928 and Barfield his *Replicit* and *Autem* (further observations) early in 1929. Lewis probably composed his *Replies to Objections* and *Note on the Law of Contradiction* by the early summer of 1929, for from then until September he stayed at Belfast helping to nurse his father, who lay dying of cancer.

The *Summa*, *Replicit*, *Autem*, *Note* and *Replies* are all paginated in sequence. Just when Lewis wrote his fifteen-page essay on morality, *De Bono et Malo*, is a matter for conjecture. The break in pagination and notably more Christian tone (for instance, the name "God" used interchangeably with "Spirit") suggest 1930 rather than 1929. The period from October, 1929, to the end of 1931 proved a watershed in Lewis's life, one of psychological integration very evident in his letters after his father's death had enabled him to purchase his permanent resident, "The Kilns." This integration was completed by his acceptance of Anglicanism in 1931.

In *De Bono et Malo* Lewis set out to refute Steiner's antinomian postulate of an "inner law-giver" by asserting his own Kantian ethic in which—not surprisingly in his recent circumstances—duty took precedence over all other moral imperatives. As a counterblast, Barfield wrote his treatise *De Toto et Parte*, expounding an ethic of self-realisation that he expected Lewis to dispute. After penning a rather acerbic page or two under the heading *Commentarium in De Toto et Parte*, Lewis lost interest. By 1932 he was devising the rapidly-written *Pilgrim's Regress*, in which the figure History suggested by Barfield's historicism, appears among characters typifying erroneous beliefs. He resisted all efforts to persuade him either to resume the "war" or adapt the Summa to his new Christian framework, explaining some years later "I wish I could Christianise the *Summa* but.... When a truth has ceased to be a mistress for pleasure and become a wife for fruit it is almost unnatural to go back to the dialectic ardours of the wooing."[13]

In an essay he probably wrote before *De Toto*, Barfield distinguished two strains of Romanticism.[14] The first, "the pursuit of ... pure Romance ... the cult of far away and long ago," had fascinated Lewis ever since, at sixteen, he had begun devouring fantasies by George Macdonald and William Morris while undergoing private tuition at Gerat Bookham. In the long letters Lewis began writing in 1914 to his friend Arthur Greeves back in Ireland, rationalism co-exists with the cult of Celtic myths, Arthurian legends and Victorian romances. The rationalism became more explicit under the influence of the tutor, W. T. Kirkpatrick. To find Lewis one day revelling nostalgically in a Morris romance and another day denouncing the "already decaying superstition" of Christianity with its "tomfoolery" of Virgin Birth and "magic healings" is like discovering a woodland cottage illuminated by twilight without and fluorescence within.[15] No extant account conveys the full vehemence of Lewis's attacks upon Greeves's Christian beliefs and of his denunciations of his own father. Ultimately religious conversion integrated the romantic and rational aspects of Lewis's personality, in which the Dreamer, entranced by Macdonald and Morris, and the Mentor, admiring Gibbon, Johnson and Jane Austen, had dwelt together as neighbours not on speaking terms.

The second strain of Romanticism described by Barfield is metaphysical idealism, giving rise to "a new theory of poetry, which it sees for the first time more as a religion than a pastime." Undoubtedly the author of *Poetic*

Diction is a Romantic in this sense. His friendship with Lewis has been likened to that of Coleridge with Wordsworth.[16] The mutually sustaining rivalry of the "Great War" could only have continued between young scholars who shared a common background and set of values. Like Lewis a solicitor's son, Barfield had been brought up as an agnostic and had taken a Classics scholarship from Highgate School to Wadham. Because he read English for the full three years, he wrote more sensitively than Lewis on poetic imagery and rhythm, but profited greatly from the latter's classical learning and skill in logic. Had not the Depression obliged him to join the family law firm, he would undoubtedly have produced *What Coleridge Thought* far earlier than 1971, for the financial crash cut off funds intended to sponsor Barfield's visit to America to edit Coleridge's prose works. The demands of legal practice left him time only to write the essays printed in *Romanticism Comes of Age*, including a paper on Coleridge completed in 1932. His achievement during two scholarly careers—before and after his quarter-century of legal practice—lies in that nameless and little-explored region where philosophy, etymology and critical theory meet.

In dedicating *Poetic Diction* to "Clive Hamilton," Barfield used a Blake aphorism: "Opposition is true friendship." Lewis's "opposition," as Barfield remarks, "proved a major spring of energy for the book." Lewis put at his service not only his learning but the critical and logical facility acquired under Kirkpatrick's exacting tutorship and developed through the "Greats" programme. For example, when Barfield criticized syllogistic reasoning about objects considered out of context, and proposed a principle of "polarity" permitting objects to display opposed properties, like positive and negative charges, Lewis penned an elaborate *Note on the Law of Contradiction*. Driven to define "polarity" more carefully, Barfield subsequently elaborated his now well-known concept of "polar logic" to replace the "either-or" of traditional reasoning.[17] Again, when Lewis maintained, after reading Samuel Alexander's *Space, Time and Deity*,[18] that the mind could not simultaneously "enjoy" (experience) and "contemplate" its operations, Barfield was led to consider and ultimately formulate this principle, one implicit in his observation, in *Poetic Diction*, that poetic creation and appreciation or correction could not take place simultaneously.[19] At first, however, he strenuously objected to the rigidity of Lewis's "Box-and-Cox" separation of contemplation from enjoyment.

In his account of the "Great War," Lewis remarks that Barfield "changed me more than I him."[20] Not only did Lewis learn to "unthink" his twentieth-century conditioning and so become able to produce his masterpieces of historically-conscious literary interpretation, but he was influenced by Barfield's arguments even where he refused to change his mind. Despite a fine passage on imagination in the *Summa*, he continued to insist that imagination conveyed meaning, not truth. Nevertheless he based his fiction— the Narnia tales, the planetary romances, supremely *Till We Have Faces*— on the assumption that divine truth enters the human psyche via myth, dream or other manifestation of imagination. Again, the landscapes and climates of Narnia harmonize with the prevailing turn in the action and thus demonstrate Barfield's central theory, best expressed in *Saving the Appearances*, that early man's "primal participation" in nature was inevitably followed by a detachment necessary to develop powers of analysis and that this in turn would lead to an impending era of "self-conscious participation." M. H. Abrams has brilliantly explored this "metaphysical" strain of Romanticism in *Natural Supernaturalism*.

Even though Lewis, during and after the "Great War", insisted on the absoluteness of ethical imperatives, his late *Studies in Words* seems at one point to imply a shift towards belief in an "inner lawgiver."[21] On historical determinism, too, he wavered, as Barfield has demonstrated in a recent essay "C. S. Lewis and Historicism."[22] On the one hand, each man separately journeys towards or away from heaven; on the other hand, God spent some centuries hammering into Jewish heads his oneness and demand for righteousness.[23] Barfield cites *Perelandra* on primal living Nature giving place to a modern cosmos rationally understandable but devoid of life and meaning. Furthermore, Lewis's memorable reconstruction of the medieval cosmos in *The Discarded Image* implies a subsequent shift in human consciousness. So does his exposure, in *A Preface to Paradise Lost*, of the fallacy of the "unchanging human heart."[24] Yet, as Barfield shrewdly comments, "the very notion of change or development seemed alien to Lewis."[25]

Having demonstrated the importance of the "Great War" controversies, I ought logically to publish the letters and essays with appropriate introduction and commentary. For several reasons this cannot be done. The *Summa* manuscript, which remains in Mr Barfield's possession, will doubtless be sold and separately published. The letters by Lewis will presumably appear in the three-volume collection now being prepared by his biographer Walter Hooper. Manuscripts by Mr Barfield will form part of his estate. The following study of the letters, the essays, and a difficult but rewarding diagram on the origin of grammar and logic, that Mr. Barfield intended to use but never mailed, is intended to elucidate the controversy and set it against its background in the history of ideas.

17

The reader may find to his surprise that the disputants seem to consider themselves philosophers rather than literary scholars. Lewis, in particular, had developed a philosopher's precision under his unbelieving "logic-engine" of a private tutor,[26] had studied Philosophy for four years and only taken an English degree because openings in Philosophy were few and far between. Even afterwards, he had taught Philosophy for a year. This may explain why he took seven years to produce his first significant critical article[27] and ten to complete *The Allegory of Love*. Many a North American university would have denied him tenure, but in Oxford's more tolerant climate he had time to engage in these controversies while coping with a heavy load of tutoring and winning an unpleasant battle against the college president to secure admission of students on intellectual merit.[28] His psychological liberation after he had made peace first with his earthly and then with his heavenly father and entered the Anglican church becomes very evident in the magnificently concrete imagery of the letters he wrote to Greeves describing the woodland and wild life near his new home. Even by the end of 1929, a "blessed sense of charity" enabled him to think humorously rather than angrily of collegiate opponents.[29]

Such an outpouring of critical and creative writing followed the relief of Lewis's various tensions that only by an effort of "unthinking" can we realise how much larger Barfield must have loomed in the nineteen-twenties. Neither of the two slim volumes of verse Lewis had published under his pseudonym had sold well, despite a favourable review of *Dymer* (1926), his psychological epic.[30] After the latter volume failed, he composed a long "Document" analysing away his motives for desiring success as an author.[31] Barfield, by contrast, had under his own name published two books. *History in English Words* had attracted comment, mainly favourable, in well-known journals on each side of the Atlantic, while before the last shots of the "Great War" *Poetic Diction* was praised at some length in the *Times Literary Supplement*.[32] Any observer at that time must have expected the name of Barfield, rather than Lewis, to become a household word. That the rather chilly young don who wrote the *Summa* should have become so versatile an author and the recipient of countless letters from admiring readers can be accounted for by the wide appeal of his chosen genres. He could not, however, have developed as religious apologist, novelist or literary historian and expounder of the medieval *Weltanschauung* but for the stimulus of his controversies with Barfield.

The investigation that has sent me to a variety of philosophers from Plato and Aristotle to Croce, Alexander and, of course, Steiner has shown that

Lewis's tribute to his "unofficial teacher" was no exaggeration. Certainly, Barfield's subject-matter can never assure him of so wide a readership as Lewis enjoyed, and his style, graceful and incisive as it is, lacks Lewis's compelling analogies and conversational rhythms. Yet a careful reading of his contributions to the "Great War" and, still more, his published works, suggests at least the possibility that Barfield's ideas may in the future be found the more original and more seminal.

CHAPTER 2

The Armoury

In a full edition of the "Great War" the disputants' innumerable allusions and formidable background reading could be made clear through annotation and commentary. Their intellectual weaponry consists of a few standard plays and poems—notably *Hamlet*, *The Tempest* and *Prometheus Unbound*—but of philosophical texts ranging over two millennia. It seems best, therefore, to deal first with the most relevant arguments in *Poetic Diction* and in those works by Steiner that Barfield had read, indicating philosophical sources in each case. Next Lewis's own ideas, in the *Summa* and *De Bono et Malo*, and finally Barfield's from *De Toto* onwards, will be considered in relation to their apparent sources.

I

After half a century, *Poetic Diction* retains a freshness, power of suggestion and richness of illustration and image that no outline could convey. Some reminder of its main argument is needed, however, as a preliminary to discussion of the controversy arising from this, Barfield's best-known and most fruitful work of criticism.

First, Barfield argues from several examples that poetic language induces a "felt change of consciousness" in the reader, thereby causing him to grow in knowledge, wisdom and the imaginative power to perceive resemblances. Poetic metaphors restore a primal unity between perceiving subject—in this case the reader—and experienced object. Barfield's favourite example, the Greek word *pneuma*, originally connoted "wind," "breath" and "spirit,"[1] now denoted separately in consequence of modern man's analytic thinking and detachment from Nature. Primal man unreflectingly experienced a world no less alive than himself, hence expressed his experience in figurative, or "poetic" language. Then mythology, "the ghost of concrete meaning,"[2] peopled heaven and earth with living spirits. Daily Hyperion warmed Gē (Earth), and annually Demeter sprang up in the cornfield. Barfield, like any anthroposophist, claims that ancient man neither invented the gods nor projected human feelings into a meaningless cosmos, but expressed a life and meaning inherent in Nature.

After the rational or "prosaic" principle had begun to divide meanings into physical and non-physical denotative words and detach human consciousness from its cosmic source, the old undivided meanings struggled on in Plato's Forms (Ideas). The categories of Aristotle and the Scholastics completed the sundering process; then Nominalism obliterated any vestigial links between thoughts and things.

The earliest poems, not appreciated as such, conveyed lived experience by imitative sounds and rhythms. In time the "given" meanings of words gave way to meanings "achieved" in poetic metaphors. In his thesis Barfield followed a single word, "ruin," from its original connotations down to its various uses by Shakespeare and later poets to show how given meanings flow on beneath current denotations and resurge at times when poets strive to freshen poetic diction by returning to "Nature."[3]

A modern poet therefore fights against the drift of words towards single meanings and abstraction. He first creates by allowing experience to well up from his unconscious, then corrects and re-orders the potential poem lying before him. Such revision demands an appreciative power of contrary nature to the original creative urge.

Since the discursive intellect forever dries up meanings, modern language abounds in dead metaphors, indeed is "fossil poetry."[4] Calling great poetry "the progressive incarnation of life in consciousness,"[5] Barfield insists that pleasure is not its object but its test, for the initial "felt change of consciousness" precedes awareness of the poem as process rather than completed artefact.

In his illuminating Appendices, Barfield traces the abstractness of modern "prosaic" diction and thought to Locke and Kant. He holds the latter, widely revered as "the Aristotle of post-Christian thought,"[6] responsible for the belief that thoughts arise subjectively from neural activity. From Kant, who defined thinking as constituting rather than merely including an act of judgment, flows a stream of "aesthetic" critics, supremely Croce, who by divorcing art from knowledge have devalued poetry to the level of meaningless emotion. To understand the primitive mind, says Barfield, we must "unthink" our now conventional distinction between subject and object, self and world. Whenever we think creatively rather than passively understanding, that distinction in any case disappears.

In the chapter Barfield added by request of his publishers, he gave further examples of words becoming abstract.[7] He also threw out some interesting ideas that had occurred to him independently of Lewis's influence. One is a definition of poetic criticism as "midwifery," bringing the reader from being aware of the finished poem to imaginatively participating in its creation.

21

Another is the need to trace words to their figurative origins so as to "unthink" that "parochial" distinction between poetry and science responsible for the Crocean view of poetry as meaningless emotion.[8] Most important is Barfield's distinction between man as maker and as knower. The poetic (i.e. "making" or creative) principle produces original art and real advances in knowledge. The prosaic (i.e. rational) principle at best produces understanding rather than knowledge, and at worst leads to pedantry or fact-collecting. Nevertheless it makes possible individual consciousness. The conscious self must identify with life, through "poetry" in the sense of imaginative or creative activity, or else philosophy must come to a standstill. Barfield's savage attack upon logical positivism in the Preface to the 1952 edition arose from his conviction that linguistic analysis based upon fixed and static denotations represented the triumph of the prosaic principle, Blake's "ratio" and "single vision."

Only this chapter distinguishes the book from the thesis. Lewis denied that ancient poetry had conveyed knowledge rather than pleasure and emphatically rejected any claim that either the dream-like awareness of primal poets or the imaginative vision of modern poets could embody truth, as distinct from emotion, illusion or downright fiction. Thus the contestants arrived at their central and creative disagreement: whether subject and object were ever one or always distinct. Lewis maintained the poet's separateness from, and health-giving requirement to attend to, the object. Barfield has persistently and with increasing elaboration argued the case for the underlying oneness of subject and object, sometimes by adducing evidence of the human body's material identity with its environment, sometimes by pointing to modern notions of matter, mind and feelings as systems of opposed energies or impulses.

Any student of romantic poetry will recognise the echoes of Blake, Wordsworth and Coleridge in *Poetic Diction*. He needs some acquaintance with philosophy to understand why Barfield blamed the imbalance between poetic and prosaic language upon Kant and Croce, and why the thesis prompted the disputants to argue about the One and the Many, Being and Becoming and other issues in Greek philosophy. He would need a close acquaintance with Lewis's published and unpublished writings to realise how the thesis marshalled Lewis's thoughts the way that they were going.

Lewis made a fundamental contribution to Barfield's intellectual development by pointing out the parallel between the contrast of "poetic" with "prosaic" thinking and Aristotle's concepts of active and passive reason (*poiein* and *paschein*). In a letter Lewis notes having "got the poetic and the other mind settled," then supplies the substantial extract from *De Anima* that appears (together with a Coleridge quotation) as frontispiece to *Poetic Diction*.[9] This antithesis, together with another one originally considered by Aristotle, that between Knowing and Knowledge, underpin the book's whole edifice. If knowing be a creative act by which one orders and explains experience, one therefore reasons actively. If knowledge be a body of fact (Coleridge's "fixities and definities"), to be "seen," "grasped" or "absorbed" —physical metaphors are unavoidable—the learner reasons passively. In the chapter substantially quoted by Barfield,[10] Aristotle distinguishes between an active intelligence employed by the mathematician to apprehend truths inaccessible to the senses and a passive intelligence that, fed and activated by sense-impressions, subordinates the mind to data ("things given"). Active reason produces concepts and, because it subsists unaided by the senses, constitute man's immortal aspect, while passive reason produces percepts and dies with the body it depends on. Similarly Barfield, writing without then having read *De Anima*, defines as "poetic" the language that quickens into life whatever objects or experiences the poet's mind acts upon, and as "prosaic" the language employing words denotatively and in fixed order. Poetic language forever creates new metaphors and explores new connotations; prosaic language employs dead metaphors in literal or even abstract senses.

To reason thus is to employ Plato's distinction between Being, the property of the "real" world of Forms, and Becoming, the activity of the "phenomenal" world perceived by the senses.[11] This world of appearances, in its ceaseless interchange of action and suffering, is to its unchanging and un-created Cause as opinion to certain knowledge.[12] As God eternally is and the world forever becomes, so man's reason immortality is and his feelings and appetites, for this life's span, form part of the world's phenomenal flux and therefore of its Becoming.[13] Barfield reverses Plato's order of precedence by treating poetic language, an eternal becoming, as equal or superior to prosaic or static language. In the *Summa*, however, Lewis follows Plato in considering Spirit (his term for Being) superior to souls, which have the property of Becoming.

In discussing myth, the source of poetic language, Barfield combines Platonic and Aristotelian modes of thought. Myth, which pre-dates our distinction between inner and outer reality (subjective and objective), points back to the undivided reality primal man directly apprehended. The bifurcative tendency that gave rise to separate words for "spirit," "breath" and "wind" operates not only in etymological but, as Barfield has since pointed out, in biological evolution. Already, in *History in English Words*, he had traced "separative projection"[14] at work to produce individual self-awareness.

By denying reality to Plato's Forms, Barfield suggests, Aristotle began the process or sundering inner, "imaginary" experience from observation of outer, "real" objects and events.

The nature and importance of this sundering becomes clearer in the light of Aristotle's distinction—implicit in *Poetic Diction*, therefore much discussed in the "Great War"—between potency (*dynamis*) and actuality (*energeia*).[15] The formless substance (*hylē*) of matter cannot progress from potency to actuality until it be activated or impregnated by form (*eidos*).[16] Thus the body cannot realise its potential life without the soul, which has life actually. In *Poetic Diction* Barfield portrays poetic diction as the means by which poets give form to the *hylē* of events and sensations. In his earlier book he discerns in evolving language the form of emerging human consciousness. *Poetic Diction* unites the Platonic concept of a Becoming inherent in language with the Aristotelian concept of a potential meaning in reality (inner and outer) that poetic imagination makes actual. But whereas Aristotle placed imagination low in his hierarchy of mental attributes, the post-romantic Barfield venerates it as a descendant of that primal, unself-conscious discernment of reality to which we owe the great myths. By making images, the modern poet quickens observed reality, life potential, into life actual. In prosaic language Becoming has reached final stasis. Poetic language properly conveys the excitement of Knowing; prosaic language conveys fixed Knowledge. Hence, as may be interjected, more than one scientific discovery has been explained by "poetic" metaphor or analogy before being assimiliated into a logical, "prosaic" set of laws.[17]

During the half-century since *Poetic Diction* first appeared, Barfield, like Wordsworth, has transcended the pessimism inherent in his account of primal poetry fading into the light of modern prose. This he has done by working out a concept of "polarity" he inherited from Coleridge, who derived it from Fichte and Schelling. In the face of devastating criticism from Lewis, Barfield introduced the concept during the "Great War" to show that opposed ideas, states or processes can both be valid and mutually necessary.

The Platonic and Aristotelian concepts re-worked in *Poetic Diction* underlie most philosophical positions known to Western man. Judaeo-Christian Creation accounts treat primal chaos as unrealised matter and Spirit moving on its waters as form. God exercises active reason in forming the world, man passive reason in studying His creation. As scientific humanist, T. H. Huxley sat like a child before "facts," while dismissing Spirit, or form, as unverifiable. A linguistic analyst treats words, with fixed meanings, as his data. A behaviourist, banishing mind and inner consciousness, treats behaviour as his only evidence and therefore as proper material (*hylē*) for manipulation. (He rarely seems to consider the nature and origin of any principles governing his decisions.) De Chardin, by contrast, postulates a proto-consciousness or implicit form in matter.[18] Steiner speculated on the process by which matter acquires form.[19] Knowing in the sense of "ordering" seems identical with Coleridge's Imagination, "primary" when it shapes the individual's experience into his world, "secondary" when it melts down the artist's experience to reforge it into art. Imagination fulfils the function of Aristotle's active reason and fancy that of passive reason, for Fancy reproduces experiences without fusing them and so assembles works of art unreal because "unformed."[20]

Although Lewis accepted much of the argument in the thesis before its publication, his mind worked differently from Barfield's. To him, as to Wordsworth, knowledge represented sensory experience systematized, and truth became manifest in a statement's internal consistency and fidelity to external fact. Man's mind must conform itself to nature and the language of the sense, for it perceived rather than created its environment.

II

In *Series II*, Letter II, Lewis expresses surprise at his own preoccupation with and "animosity" towards Barfield's anthroposophical beliefs. Nearly forty years later Barfield finds it no less astonishing that Lewis, of all people, could condemn Rudolf Steiner's works virtually unread.[21] Normally, scholars either become Steiner's devotees or dismiss him unread as a crank. Many prepared to accord a fair hearing to Nietzsche, nihilist and ultimately megalomaniac, will not give one to Steiner.

Nevertheless, as any serious Blake scholar must read Swedenborg, so a student of Barfield's thought, or even Lewis's, must grit his teeth and read at least those works by Steiner that Barfield had read at the time of the "Great War." The reader who squirms at the "nonsense" in *Occult Science* or the Gospel lectures—prehistoric man being brought to earth by angels, our wanderings into other worlds while asleep, the literal reading of the Gospels —would do well to make use of one of those English interpretations that seem so much clearer and more believable than Steiner's own writings, only recently well translated.[22] He could beget a tolerance by reading Steiner's unfinished autobiography. Above all, he must resolutely suspend judgment and learn to discriminate between Steiner's method of discernment, the strange things supposedly discerned, and the often admirable outcome of Steiner's teachings. However bizarre the teachings, Steiner developed his method, or "Spiritual Science," out of disciplines practised in earlier mystical traditions. A teacher who, long before our "New Consciousness" dawned, set up organic farming enterprises, expounded creative arts as therapies, developed "eurythmic" physical culture and set up programmes for both retarded and normal children that command respect among educators, deserves a fairer scrutiny than academics usually grant him.

Admittedly Steiner's writing infuriates the academic reader by its absence of documentation, its claim to authority on so many topics, its endless reiteration of the same ideas in different books, worst of all its expressed contempt for documentary evidence. Yet the social achievement of the anthroposophists—one as disproportionate to their numbers as that of an earlier deviant-Christian sect, the Quakers—the tribute Lewis paid to the characters and intellects of those anthroposophists he knew, indeed the debate he so long sustained with Barfield, constrain us to patience and willing suspension of disbelief.

Rudolf Steiner (1861-1925) enjoyed mystical experiences in childhood that left him unshakably convinced that a spiritual world existed as real as that discerned by his senses. At technical school he read precociously, even reading Kant's Critiques at fifteen. Though educated primarily in physics and biology, he tended to trace lines back into the past: from science to alchemy, from the Neoplatonists and mystics—Boehme, or pseudo-Dionysius—to Augustine, Plotinus and Plato; from the Scholastics—especially Aquinas and Erigena—to Aristotle. Taught by Brentano, he became deeply interested in Husserl: indeed his very system of spiritual training grew out of phenomenology, the study of the mind's operation.

Steiner's first creative period began when a professor compared his call for attention to thinking, as distinct from things thought, to Goethe's remarks on how colour had developed from its invisible source, light.[23] By the age of twenty-three, Steiner was invited to Weimar to catalogue and edit Goethe's scientific writings. His reading of Goethe, prompted by the professor's comparison, bore fruit in *Goethes Weltanschauung* (1897).

Steiner's next creative period began with his conversion to Christianity, about the turn of the century, while he was editing a Berlin literary journal. Brought up a free-thinker, Steiner had attacked the Christian ethic in *The Philosophy of Freedom* (1894), stigmatizing the Kantian categorical imperative as a "philistine embodiment of duty in an external code."[24] Since, he maintained, no "world dictator" governs human actions, man must claim his freedom to work out his own moral decisions. Hitherto Steiner had been influenced mainly by Goethe, Nietzsche and Schiller.

Steiner always used his dead selves as stepping-stones. His virtually existentialist belief in a moral freedom based on disciplined thinking, feeling

26

and willing became blended with new insights gained from reading Christian and Hindu scriptures. During the first decade of this century he presided over the German branch of the Theosophical Society but was expelled for refusing to subscribe to Annie Besant's proclamation of the boy seer Krishnamurti as Christ re-incarnate.[25]

Steiner gave his lecture-courses on the Gospels during the turmoil preceding his foundation of the Anthroposophical Society (1913). They reflect his refusal to confine enlightenment to oriental mystics, his insistence that western tradition supplies similar insights, and that the Incarnation both consummated all religious teaching and gave meaning to man's entire history.

Knowledge of Higher Worlds and *Occult Science* embody respectively Steiner's way of discernment and the things he discerned. He defined Anthroposophy as "a path of knowledge which leads from Spirit in Man to Spirit in the Universe."[26] Anthroposophical training reunites the human ego, "of the same nature and essence as the divine,"[27] with the external world from which it has become separated, a cosmos not less spiritual than material. Reuniting subject and object involves making "the world-content into our thought-content" and conversely knowing external Nature by learning "to know her within us."[28] This demands above all humility and reverence both for Nature and the psyche. Next it demands attention to our acts of thinking and making moral choices, rather than to the thoughts and moral laws themselves. Freedom to think and decide results from contemplating oneself as object while opening oneself also to external impressions.

In his first stage, the prospective "initiate" trains his *imagination* by focussing his thoughts upon some object having no personal associations for him. Steiner's favourite example was a seed. Ultimately the mediator becomes aware of formative, or "etheric" forces producing growth in himself as in the seed and attains an ordered vision of his own past development.

After training himself in "systematic imagination" the initiate enters his second stage, *inspiration*. As in oriental disciplines, he must empty both mind and heart, so that their emptiness may be filled by awareness of the "astral" forces that form human feelings and relationships. Having come to distinguish truth from illusion, he learns to view himself as "a link in the whole of life"[29] and undergoes purifications metaphorically represented as "fire, water and air": suffering, withdrawal of support, and dependence on his inner resources.[30] He who would discern that spiritual element informing all human relationships must renounce egoism, competitive striving and the propensity to use people. He must also attend to normally involuntary functions: thinking, resolving, and especially purposive speech and action. The seeker fully

27

open to impressions from others can enjoy a vision of the entire human drama—past, present and perhaps to come.

Having in this "inspiration" (breathing-in) stage developed feeling to its utmost, the initiate now develops *intuition* by exerting his *will* to relate to those spiritual forces responsible for cosmic, as distinct from personal and historical, evolution. Because he has become detached from self, home and kindred, his soul's three fundamental forces, thinking, feeling and willing are now in balance. Having attained an equilibrium, the lack of which would produce such personality disorders as cold calculation, unbridled passion, sentimentalism, tyranny or impulsiveness, the seeker has completed his "initiation."[31] The new-born "higher" or immortal self enjoys clairvoyant awareness of both the natural and social worlds and their spiritual ground. Like Wordsworth he "sees into the life of things" and like the prophet of old remains still and knows God. Faith has "vanished into knowledge, which nothing can undermine."[32]

To understand Steiner's teaching, it is essential to realise that he claims objective validity for his insights. By focussing upon the thinking process rather than upon sense-data, he asserts, he has attained a form of organised knowledge complementary to that accruing from the natural sciences. As anyone with the requisite training can verify a scientific experiment, so, says Steiner, anyone who follows the anthroposophical discipline can attain the same "supersensible" knowledge.

That knowledge itself comes as a result of a training that represents a backwards retracing of human social evolution. As the ancient myths show, primal man enjoyed clairvoyant perception of the natural world and its spiritual ground. As intuitive awareness weakened, initiates in Mystery-centres preserved spiritual knowledge in myths and oracular teachings, having first entered the spiritual world by the death-like trances still practised by Hindu holy men. As man separated himself from the natural world, prophets transmitted external inspiration, as from Mount Sinai. Christ countered the corruption of fallen man by initiating disciples who could remain fully conscious. Thus He opened initiation to all men, permitting them to retain self-awarness so that they could relate to each other in willed love, *Agapē*, rather than the *Eros* of family or kinship ties. The Fall had come about through attacks by "Ahrimanic" beings upon man's spiritual awareness, his "etheric" body, and by "Luciferic" beings upon his social awareness, his "astral" body. The Fall exposed the human spirit to destruction through materialism and self-serving passion, yet made possible human freedom and dignity.[33]

What concerns us here is not Steiner's system of spiritual training, his "Western occultism," nor his complex account of a supposed course of planetary and human evolution, but his psychology. The human body, in the extended sense common in medieval and renaissance psychology, is physical, etheric and astral. The child recapitulates the first age of man by developing its structure of bone and muscle. By puberty the "etheric" body, the pattern of nerves and reflexes, has developed. The "astral" body of characteristic social attitudes and feelings develops during adolescence. Finally develops the Ego or self-consciousness, the soul.[34]

Steiner's account of the further "ages of man," during which the intellect and spirit develop, becomes clear only in the light of his account of the "evolution of consciousness" that the individual recapitulates. During ancient Near and Middle Eastern civilisations, man separated from the spiritual world to form his "Sentient Soul" of characteristic feelings and responses. The Graeco-Roman culture saw the birth of his Intellectual Soul, the capacity for reasoning and abstraction. The era of the Intellectual Soul lasted from Plato to Aquinas. Since the fifteenth century the Consciousness Soul has evolved.[35]

The resultant detachment of the individual Ego from Nature and from collective thinking and feeling enabled natural science to flourish. Just as each era has ended in a time of troubles preceding a new advance, so each phase of individual growth—infancy, childhood, adolescence—ends in a period of instability. Steiner draws parallels between the eras of human history and the phases of human life.

Modern man, he says, is undergoing temptation by Luciferic powers appealing to his passions and by Ahrimanic powers dangling the lure of technological materialism. Should man succumb, he will enter upon a Darwinian struggle for existence, in all its untempered greed and egoism. Should man be delivered by the knowledge of his spiritual origin and destiny, he will regain primal clairvoyance while preserving individual self-consciousness.[36]

I have tried to abstract from an idea-system as vast and complex as, say Freudian psychology, just those teachings that furnished cause of conflict between Barfield and Lewis: the spiritual training, the tutelary and demonic spirits, the pattern discerned in history and individual life, the cultivation of self-awareness and attention to the mind's functioning. For Steiner's teachings concerning planetary evolution, the life of Christ, future eras and re-incarnation, the liberal and useful arts and education, the reader must consult other sources.[37] It remains to identify several general characteristics likely to have offended Lewis.

Clearly "Spiritual Science" is scientific only in a special sense. We can verify our convictions either empirically, by controlled observation or experiment, or else subjectively, in religious experience or love-relationships. A metaphysician cannot verify such statements as "I think," or "I exist," since these are matters of immediate experience and their truth has to be assumed as a preliminary to verification. None of these categories can apply to Steiner's account of cosmic and human evolution, based on facts supposedly "brought out of the spiritual world," wherein they are indelibly preserved in "Akashic records."[38] Anyone wishing to verify these assertions must submit to spiritual direction, even if this come from a book rather than a *guru*. The term "Spiritual Science" implies a parallel with empirical verification in the natural sciences, but the "initiate" discerns not a natural, historical or psychological phenomenon but its inner essence and meaning. The objectivity Steiner claims for these spiritual counterparts of phenomena may enable his apologists to bypass Popper's stipulation: "a subjective experience, or a feeling of conviction, can never justify a scientific statement," but Steiner's teachings cannot, I think, satisfy Popper's criterion: "there can be no statements in science which cannot be tested, and . . . in principle . . . refuted, by falsifying some of the conclusions which can be deduced from them."[39] While Steiner offered a means of testing his statements, it is impossible to see how statements wrongly made on the evidence of "Akashic records" could be proven false. For example, his claim that such "records" of the Gospel events renders documentary evidence unnecessary denies the basic principle of historical enquiry. We may contrast it with St. Paul's bold assertion that should the Resurrection be shown not to have occurred "then is our faith vain."[40]

To say that Steiner's teachings are not scientific is not to deny their truth or value, but only to categorise them as in essence metaphysical, hence to be judged by logical consistency and fidelity to immediate experience. The whole system depends upon two premises: that past events, activities or forms of life never disappear without trace, and that since subject and object are of the same essence there can be no clear-cut distinction between the real and the imagined. The second premise obliterates a frontier Lewis very much wanted to preserve, that between myth and historical fact, what the mind supposes and what it knows. Not only did he derive from fantasy a pleasure of a kind not derivable from history, but he had quite recently had to cope with a case in his household of raving lunacy attributable to Spiritualist beliefs. Both anthroposophical premises seem disposed of by Lewis's criticism of medieval scholars, who "find it hard to believe that anything an old *auctour* has said is simply untrue."[41]

Anthroposophy, like Theosophy, enjoyed a vogue in the Twenties. It has to this day continued to exert a minute but wholly beneficent social influence. This alone should deter us from dismissing it as an ephemeral craze arising (like Steiner's own cogitations) from dismay at the erosion of Western moral and religious values by materialism and scientific humanism. Although Anthroposophy, with its parent movement, forms part of the cultural exchange that has transplanted Marxism to the Far East and various Hindu and Buddhist cults to the West, its assertions regarding myth and cultural evolution link it with the main stream of Romantic belief so carefully traced by M. H. Abrams.

In particular, Steiner's assertion of a primal intuitive awareness of the world, followed by the alienation of human consciousness from Nature can be found in Wordsworth and many another poet or philosopher since the Enlightenment. It has even been made, in a very different form, by Marx.[42] In describing this evolution of consciousness, Barfield has generally confined himself to semantics and philosophy. The kernel of his assertion is that man, who once identified with his surroundings and therefore perceived and spoke figuratively, detached himself from those surroundings and thus could study them scientifically, but is now passing into a stage of "self-conscious participation" in Nature. This assertion, though it forms a smaller box within the Chinese box of Anthroposophy, deserves Barfield's title "Objective" Idealism because he has supported it by semantic evidence of historical shifts in human feelings and awareness that can, in principle, be falsified.

III

Lewis never expressed scepticism concerning the primal intuitive awareness assumed by both Barfield and Steiner. His permanent discomfort at Steiner's teaching stems rather from disbelief in truth supposedly apprehended by the imagination, together with an extravert distrust of the notions of thinking about thinking and souls exposed to scrutiny. Moreover Steiner's assertion of the trained soul's freedom to act out its moral intuitions distressed him. Steiner's claim to have crossed the gap between subject and object and alone penetrated the obscurity of the prehistoric past aroused that distrust of authority that Lewis, as a scholar, found so hard to overcome during his own progress towards Christian orthodoxy. He ridiculed Steiner's ideas concerning physical, etheric and astral bodies and the soul's survival in a non-material environment. He incessantly chastised the folly of submitting to training that would disclose not the reality behind the phenomena but only further and delusory phenomena, a *"Chimaerarum terra"* (*Series I*, Letter I, sketch).

For the constructive, as distinct from the dissuasive, arguments in his *Summa*, Lewis drew most heavily upon Samuel Alexander's *Space, Time and Deity*. In this difficult but at that time new and influential set of Gifford Lectures, Alexander was expounding a kind of emergent evolution of mind from neural reactions, and of deity from mind. Neural reactions, he suggested, came about by reason of the "nisus" or creative tendency causing space-time to engender matter, matter to engender life and living structures to engender mind.[43]

Though Lewis often discusses space-time in the *Summa*, his replaces this as a term for the Absolute by "Spirit," a term common to various idealist philosophers from Hegel to Croce. Subsequently Lewis rejected Alexander's emergent evolutionism,[44] but always valued the contemplation-enjoyment distinction made early in the book.[45] Alexander states that each individual *contemplates* external objects, or his fellow-men, but *enjoys* his own sensations and feelings. His knowledge, therefore, consists in the "compresence" of mind and external object. Space-time has brought forth this "categorial" or universal feature, the body-mind relationship we enjoy. Philosophy treats essentially of categorial rather than "empirical," or variable, features. In the *Summa*, Lewis likewise employs "empirical" to denote "transitory" or "incidental."

As he explains in his autobigraphy, Lewis found Alexander's assertion that the mind could not in the same moment enjoy and contemplate very true to his own experience. By trying as he had done to re-live ecstatic moments or experiences (given the class-name "Joy"), he had, as he realised, attempted at once to enjoy and contemplate them. An example probably familiar to most readers would be Miriam's effort, in Lawrence's *Sons and Lovers*, to enjoy yet also contemplate her ecstatic communion with Nature.

Lewis, a kindred spirit to Alexander, turned the distinction into a moral principle. As Alexander's matter by indwelling creativeness brings forth mind, so Lewis's "Spirit" hastens to embody itself in matter, and the human spirit in artefacts. Again, both authorship and literary appreciation demand an interplay between enjoyment of our feelings or sensations, and contemplation of objects outside ourselves. Like Alexander, Lewis therefore condemns introspection.[46] Eventually he divided all experience into three categories: the enjoyed, the contemplated and the unconscious.

Inasmuch as "enjoyed" and "contemplated" imply no claim that the one is more real than the other, they may prove more useful for the literary critic than "subjective" and "objective," but, as Lewis points out, they are not equivalent. The universal creative Spirit (Lewis's pantheistic term for "God") is "pure subject," but to "see as Spirit sees" is to view all things with utter comprehension and objectivity. We can enjoy but not contemplate Spirit: that is, we cannot behold it entire from without, as it can us. Again, we contemplate other people yet may not view them objectively. The more, indeed, we can share or imagine their perspective, the more fully and fairly we comprehend them, but only Spirit sees them at once with total insight and total objectivity.

Space, Time and Deity played a key role alike in Lewis's argument with Barfield and in his own development. If the mind enjoyed its thoughts and sensations but contemplated only other beings and objects, then to cultivate self-consciousness was to defy the course of nature. Moreover, as Lewis was to learn from Barfield, Spirit could best enjoy human nature by becoming flesh, and man could no more comprehend Spirit than a character could comprehend the dramatist who created him. The elaborate analogies Lewis drew in the *Summa* between Spirit's relations with human souls and those of an author with his characters constituted an unrecognized rehearsal of his own duel with the Christian God, even of his own role as a popular apologist. Alexander, like Lewis after him, illustrated several points by allusions to *Hamlet*.[47] He dubbed his ethic "natural piety,"[48] though he used Wordsworth's phrase to signify acceptance of observed natural realities as "categorial" and final.

The Stoic, even Manichean ethos of the *Summa* owes much to Kant. The teaching of Kant's *Critique of Practical Reason* permeates *Summa* Book II, "Value."[49] Like Kant, Lewis enjoins the distinterested pursuit of good, regardless of religious hope or fear. Like Kant, he considers "supersensible" knowledge beyond human attainment, refuses to represent duties as divine commands, and grounds hope in reason rather than divine assurance. Lewis does not directly discuss the "categorical imperative," but the principle of acting in universally valid ways underlies his ethos of regarding one's situation "as Spirit sees it." Both in the *Summa* and in *De Bono et Malo* he endorses Kant's distinction between the theoretical sphere of knowledge and the more important practical sphere of moral action. *De Bono* has the puritan flavour of Kant's teaching, inasmuch as it gives highest priority to duty performed regardless of inclination.

Lewis drew upon Aquinas not only for the titles and forms of his *Summa*, *Replies to Objections* and *De Bono et Malo*[50] but for some fundamental principles. One is that to define an entity is not to prove its existence, though it is a pre-requisite to proof.[51] Unlike Aquinas, however, Lewis denies the possibility of imageless thinking and essences not knowable in experience. He profoundly agrees with St. Thomas in judging an act by its intention rather than its consequence, in finding virtuous action the less commendable for being undertaken in passion, and in thinking evil not positive but "privative," an absence of good.[52] Above all, Lewis grounds his whole case in the "Great War" letters on a principle Aquinas insistently maintained, that truth or falsehood can be predicated only of intellectual judgments, never of things imagined.

Finally, Lewis owed to Benedetto Croce several important arguments in the letters and the *Summa*. At that time, Croce's ideas on Aesthetics and his book *The Philosophy of the Spirit* were much discussed in Oxford.[53] Our only direct evidence that Lewis read Croce is his explanation, in reply to Barfield's query, of Croce's distinction between aesthetic experience and what Croce considers the inferior pleasure afforded by a natural scene. Though in the letter Lewis disagrees with Croce's view that the reality of an object is irrelevant to its enjoyment, he argues in the *Summa* that to prove a myth true would destroy its value.

Lewis's whole view of poetry in the "Great War" implies his assent to the Crocean definition of poetry as "pure lyrical intuition,"[54] a definition rejected in *Poetic Diction*. Croce takes up the eighteenth-century philosopher Vico's postulate of a "poetic" mode of consciousness preceding the "rational" mode in order to trace the manifestations of a "Spirit" somewhat like Alexander's "nisus." Spirit first appears in the Aesthetic mode, in the poet's awareness of particulars. Next, Spirit becomes more evident in its Logical and Ethical modes, and completely manifest in History, the full expression of man's self-realisation. On this model, Lewis erected his own more complex hierarchy of modes of the spiritual life, to which he devotes some memorable sections of the *Summa*.

Lewis undoubtedly agreed with Croce (and Vico) that a work of art can be understood and judged only within its historical context. He also agreed that no valid assertions can be made about "art" or "poetry," only about paintings or poems. Quite probably he agreed with Croce's Shelleyan assertion that a poem, because it proceeds from "lyrical intuition," exists when mentally composed rather than when printed. He certainly shared Croce's opinion regarding the nature of poetry, though he might have modified its expression. Supposed genres, said Croce, all manifest the lyrical mode, which implies two elements: a complex of images (of persons, gestures, etc.), and a feeling that animates those images. Poetry differs from Philosophy in producing myth rather than logical statement, from History and Science in being concerned with words, images or states of mind rather than facts, and from Ethics in having no intended consequence, no palpable design upon us.[55]

As will be seen, Lewis begins his onslaught on Barfield's arguments in *Poetic Diction* from a definition of imagination as images together with a "mental complex" about them. Insistently he opposes Barfield's philosophical realism, the belief in Truth beyond "true assertions." Equally firmly he denies Barfield's inference of an evolution of language from figurative to abstract. A contributory cause of Lewis's inconsistency about progress in history may well be that he sympathised with Croce's rejection of any metaphysical or teleological explanation of history, though as a Christian he was bound to accept one. While Barfield could share Croce's view of a historical evolution of human consciousness, he could never believe that evolution to be without purpose.

IV

If one theme has been uppermost in Barfield's critical and philosophical writing, it is the relationship between a man's inner self and the surrounding world. He has always denied that absolute frontier between subject and object that Lewis always affirmed. Coleridge endlessly brooded upon this barrier and Steiner claimed to have crossed it, by meditating upon a perceived object so as to sink himself into it. By this process, Steiner claimed, he could gaze upon what Goethe called *Urphänomene*, the realities beheld clairvoyantly by primal man.[56] At the time of the "Great War," Barfield had not long been reading Steiner, and so occupied a no-man's land between Coleridge's survey and Steiner's supposed crossing. In the *Critique of Pure Reason* Kant had declared the *Ding an sich*, or "thing-in-itself," unknowable,[57] so that Lewis felt bound to accept phenomena, literally "appearances," as the best available substitute for knowledge. As an anthroposophist, Barfield believed the *Ding an sich* knowable through a training he had not yet completed.

When Barfield later described his principal contribution to the debate, *De Toto et Parte*, as "very Coleridgean,"[58] he referred not merely to the title but to the tractate's pervading organicism. This can be traced much further back than Coleridge. Augustine treats of God as universal whole, reflected throughout His creation, in that each part forms a subsidiary whole.[59] In Augustine also may be found the anthroposophical postulate of spiritual organs of discernment, and the image of spirit and wind as expressing a dichotomy between subject and object.[60] The example of words bifurcating from a single root, *pneuma*, figures so largely in Barfield's thought because his central interest lies in this relationship between man's inner consciousness and the apparently external world. The "nisus" of language both reflects and in its way contributes to this separation. In the "Great War" he uses Steiner's favourite motif, the comparison of human growth to a seed becoming a flower, but in his published writings has passed beyond analogy. In *Roman-*

35

ticism Comes of Age, he adopts the medieval notion of truth as not a copy of an object but the object reforming itself in the subject's mind. In the 1951 Preface to *Poetic Diction*, he relates the first use of the atomic bomb to the destructive energy within the human mind. The re-forming process as between one human mind and another he expresses, in the "Great War," in the Greek concept of a *tokos* by which words take root in another's mind as thoughts. (This, of course, lies behind Shelley's famous lines in the "Ode to the West Wind.")

Barfield's thought therefore includes the Romantic concepts of organicism and dynamism, but his inspiration comes from further back. Like Aquinas he thinks of the world, and the Spirit's formative work therein, existentially, as purposive striving. Aquinas, however, had drawn from Aristotle the principle that all things tend to develop their potentiality (*dynamis*) into actuality (*energeia*).[61] The undeveloped potency Aristotle terms "matter" (*hylē*), and what matter acquires through being developed he terms "form" (*eidos*).

Barfield and Lewis differed not fundamentally but in emphasis. Barfield lays more stress on growth, on things or creatures becoming themselves, Lewis more on moral action, the creature fulfilling the divine will. Again, Barfield stresses the mind's creative function, its "poetic" or as Aristotle would have said its "active" intelligence, while Lewis stresses the mind's attentive or interpretative function, in Aristotle's sense its "passive" intelligence. Barfield therefore followed Steiner, Coleridge and Kant in exalting creative Reason, that forms principles, above passive Understanding, that applies them. This predilection for the biological principle of growth and reproduction perhaps explains the statement in *History in English Words* that between Aristotle and Plato lay a "great divide from which flowed in two different directions two separate streams . . . of human outlook." Barfield adds: "just as the modern European, whether or not he possesses any genuine scientific knowledge, can trace the general shape and method of his thinking" to Aristotle, "so, whether or not he calls himself a Christian," he must trace "much of his ordinary feelings . . . back to Plato."[62] Despite Lewis's humorous threat to "explode" it, this generalisation, if over-broad, becomes understandable if we think of Barfield as a natural Aristotelian and Lewis as a natural Platonist, the former concerned with life and the self as they are and can become, the latter anxious to transform both to the divine model.

Prominent in *De Toto* is the idea, which could have come from Kant or Coleridge but actually came from Steiner, that feeling and judgment occupy a middle ground between intellectual knowing and the will to act. During and since the "Great War," Barfield has attached more importance to feeling, to empathy with the object or person known, while Lewis attaches more to

36

judgment based upon analytical reasoning. Both agree to distinguish matter's chaotic multiplicity from any formal order into which our senses may organise it, but Barfield stresses more the subject's mental activity and Lewis more the object acted upon. Experience is for the one an inner spiritual or imaginative activity and for the other a disciplined attention to the world without. Naturally Barfield tends to view the world as dynamic, taking shape within the subject's mind or being reacted upon by him, Lewis to view the world as something static or "given." While each thinks the universal creative Spirit (Greek *Nous*) related to the world as artist to material, Lewis attempts to define and apply the terms he uses in philosophical or theological controversy with Thomistic rigour, while Barfield questions the terms and rules of logic themselves. This important issue in the controversy depends for its resolution upon whether Lewis is right to think of Spirit as Being, existing separately from the world in changeless relationship, or Barfield right to think of Spirit as ceaselessly generating, regenerating and acting upon a world that therefore perpetually Becomes.

PART TWO:
WAR GAMES

CHAPTER 3

The "Great War" Letters

The current cliché "War Games," chosen as title for the ensuing survey of the whole series of letters and tractates, may help us to view the controversies as manoeuvres rather than a fight to the death. If the friends continued to disagree on several important issues, against scientific materialists, New Critics and logical positivists they remained co-belligerents. In a letter written about 1930, Lewis urges Barfield to "let the New Critics have five rounds rapid of sense." Moreover, the Letters combine the deliberateness of formal manoeuvres with the humorous badinage often exchanged between opponents on such occasions.

This deliberateness marks the item placed first in *Series I*, a four-point statement by Lewis headed "The *real* issue between us."[1]

1. *Agreed* (by you and me, also by Kant, Coleridge, Bradley, etc.) that the discursive reason always fails to apprehend reality, because it never grasps more than an abstract relational framework. The question then is whether it is possible for us to know that concrete in which alone the thing we have abstracted was real.

2. *Agreed* (by us both, and many others) that the abstract reason *plus* sense experience *plus* habits etc. gives us, in the phenomenal region, a substitute for knowledge which works tolerably well for *practical* purposes.

3. *You* maintain that this reason and experience and habit can and ought to be used to produce a knowledge of the supersensible, as confidently as it used [sic] in the sensible.

4. *I* maintain that the distinction is between the real and the phenomenal, not the sensible and supersensible. . . .

Essentially Lewis interprets Barfield's distinction between everyday "sensible" knowledge and intuitive awareness of a "supersensible" dimension as an intended Platonic contrast between phenomena ("appearances" within time and space) and reality (timeless Ideas or Forms). To underline his rebuttal, Lewis adds a series of comic sketches, each showing either himself or Barfield looking along two radiating lines representing "Sensible reality" and "Supersensible reality." The most detailed, headed "What I think you're doing," shows Barfield peering along two broken lines marked "Experience" and "Occult Science." Along the "Experience" line two human figures, the first densely-shaded and named "Reason" and the second larger and lightly-shaded and named "Sense," hold up their right arms for attention, as if waving Barfield towards "Reality" behind them. Along the "Occult Science" line Barfield peers into a region where a copse-like shape represents *"Chimaerarum Terra."* Behind that the broken but straight line becomes wavy as it passes beyond "Reason" to "Fantasia" and into the land (marked directly below "Reality") of "Nonentity." By the tree-belt, Lewis writes "Pseudo-objects generated by the schemata of reason operating without *hylē* to fill them." His objection to anthroposophical mind-training clearly echoes Bacon's to Scholastic ratiocination, and he once referred to Steiner's system as "medieval." The training, Lewis warns, will merely produce delusory appearances.

In *Series I*, Letter II, Lewis denies necessary validity to whatever may remain in the mind "after imagination." A state of poetic imagination, he asserts, "vouches only for itself," for (as he adds in a brief following letter) imagination is non-assertive, so that its images are neither true nor false as such, but non-veridical. Truth can be posited only of a judgment arrived at by comparison of any "mental complex" with the fact to which it relates.

Barfield replies in Letter IV that their "great divide" lies in this alleged difference between "fact" and related "mental complex" (later in the controversy defined as the familiar distinction of subject from object). Barfield sees Truth not as fact or known object, but as the process of knowing, "reality taking the form of consciousness." Whether this process takes place by intuition or by normal act of judgment is immaterial. Barfield terms the area of explicit logical or "sensible" awareness the "hoti-sphere" (from a Greek particle here meaning "that") in deference to Lewis's insistence upon knowledge as "knowing *that*" and "because it makes me feel grand, living as I do in Ḡolders Green[2] and not in Oxford."

By the end of Letter V, Lewis rather gleefully summarises the state of the argument as:

1. B[arfield] and L[ewis] *agree* that there is a valuable faculty called imagination—which is not the same as *imaginatio*, the image-making faculty—the exercise of which is necessary for the connaissance of meaning.

2. B. and L. *agree* that the exercise of the faculty does not enable us to make true statements or judgments (though . . . no statement . . . could be made without it).

3. B. *maintains* and L. *questions* a doctrine that this faculty produces

Truth, tho[ugh] not true statements or judgments; and that this is the only veritable Truth, "true" judgments not being really true.

4. B. *maintains* and L. *denies* a doctrine (... an interpretation of (3)) that the mind can become aware of its own activity in thinking as something other than the content or object of thought.

Next, in Letter VI, Barfield complains that (in a letter now lost) Lewis has misinterpreted an analogy comparing the realisation and formulation of truth to a plant's bearing of flowers and seeds. He continues: "the relation between imagination and *hoti* ... is analogous to the relation of a fruit or pod to its flower." Whereas he envisages a dynamic process by which reality "becomes" in the mind, his opponent thinks only of a "static" observable reality. An embryo and a man, Barfield urges, are the same "real" being at different stages. Evidently at this juncture Barfield was, in the sense expounded in *Poetic Diction*, a "poetic" thinker and Lewis a "prosaic" thinker.

Before Lewis wrote from a holiday resort the longest letter,[3] the sixteen-page Letter VII, at least one letter now lost passed in each direction. Barfield had compared the mind's awakening to reality with the erasure of colouring matter from glass, and then misunderstood Lewis's interpretation. By this time, the discussion had shifted to Barfield's account of metaphor in *Poetic Diction*.

While still unwilling to identify metaphor with poetry, Lewis admits to having under-estimated its importance. In so far as metaphor brings before the mind images or representations of objects, metaphor, he agrees, gives life to abstractions otherwise lifeless. Yet it cannot vouch for their existence, for poetry is "intensely semantic, but not at all assertive."[4] As he adds in the eighth and final letter, metaphor shows *what* an object may resemble but not *that* it exists.

Two issues preoccupy Lewis in the remainder of Letter VII and in Letter VIII. The first is how reality can assume the form of consciousness. Barfield's example will not do, for the embryo can hardly be said to *be* the man, for it becomes him whereas he never becomes it. Piquantly Lewis adds that failing further explanation Barfield will "be up against my original difficulty, that 'a donkey' and 'reality taking the form of a donkey' are all one."

The second issue recalls a comparison often made between Wordsworth and Coleridge. Like Wordsworth, Lewis simply had to believe that Nature existed outside his own mind. "If there is appearance, there is something that appears" (Letter VII). Having discomforted his opponent by suggesting during a walking-tour[5] that there might be no self but merely phenomena,

Lewis adds that if their "individual and separate selves" exist, Barfield must "either (a) assume a reality ... other than thinking, and common to us all, or (b) relapse into extreme subjective idealism ... more probably, solipsism." His humour barely concealing unease, Lewis adds that if reality be nothing more than an Ego's thinking "then the world is the content of an individual, personal *psyche*, and I (there's only one of me) may as well cut my throat tonight." A moment later, however, the letter ends in a charmingly-expressed acceptance of the dedication of *Poetic Diction*.[6]

The letters grouped as *Series II* have none of the badinage natural to fellow-lovers of Plato. Seriously, though in the main tactfully, Lewis tries to dissuade a close friend from beliefs he regards as irrational. Evidently they had been discussing Steiner's teaching upon directing one's spiritual activity. Lewis begins by distinguishing between involuntary thinking, provoked by necessity or passion, and deliberate reflection. In the latter kind, content would be governed, he suggests by one or more of four factors: (1) the thinker's conviction as to what is more and what less important; (2) a doctrine of relative importance accepted on authority; (3) the thinker's predilections for particular subject-matter, arising from temperament or environment; (4) "the natural branchings-out" of the material already pre-occupying him, "following the *leadings* of the subject" regardless of personal predilection. Lewis, who naturally prefers the fourth determinant, believes that the first might be a disguise for the third, some personal obsession. Even worse, the second may cloak the obsessional tendency of a supposed "authority," who could never be infallible. To pursue either of the first two lines of thought exclusively, Lewis warns, might cause Barfield to cut himself off from "the last chance of *rescue* from the parochialness of your own mind, or that of your age." The fourth and freest kind of thinking, he adds, "must be *kept open*" by "men of our upbringing ... whose business is ... to keep an eye upon it. When a man or an age is completely bamboozled, (4) is the only alley down wh[ich] deliverance will come."

To adapt Coleridge's remark on a Wordsworth passage, these remarks cry aloud "C. S. Lewis." They bear his hallmarks: distrust of totalitarian ideologies and twentieth-century worship of modernity; belief in humanist education as an antidote to idolatrous modernism; above all, vindication of reason when freely exercised upon material regardless of the student's own predisposition. To judge from his comment on his age's "parochialism," Lewis had by now been freed of "Chronological Snobbery" and was returning the favour.

Turning to Steiner's advice on systematic meditation, Lewis comments caustically that "no one is going to 'think about' a seed for 10 minutes on end except in obedience to a master" whose claim to authority he has tacitly accepted. "At present," Lewis continues, "the only claim that has reached me is the master's promise that if I meditate on the seed long enough I shall see blue lights or something coming round it: and your promise . . . that I shall come to see my own thinking as a being who is also everyone else's thinking, tho[ugh] he remains individual and not universal." Though neither promise proves authority, Lewis concludes, "both are verified for the sort of man who is already prepared to obey his (3)."

The same day Lewis dashed off from his rooms at Magdalen a note of apology for his final innuendo. In it he marvels at his obsessive dislike of Anthroposophy, and begs Barfield not to "bulverize this." Lewis coined the word to signify the dishonest device of substituting the imputation of motive for reasoned rejoinder. Whatever Barfield first felt about the accusation, he came to treat the matter as a joke and signed one of his tractates "Aloysius Bulver." Later on, Lewis encountered so many "bulverists" among objectors to his arguments for orthodox Christianity that he wrote an essay on the subject that deserves to be better known.[7] In Barfield, however, he discerns not the baneful influence of Freudian analysis but an innate tendency to detect manipulation, formerly by financial interests, now by Ahriman (the devil of materialism) blinding the sceptic's intellect.

Lewis debunks anthroposophical bulverism by an argument exemplifying the stand-the-enemy-on-his-head technique he later used so skilfully in his theological writing. One who believes in Ahriman can argue that denying that demon's existence is "just what it wants." How, Lewis asks, can doubt prevail when its very appearance is "hailed as the insidious approach of the enemy himself?" So belief can be "built up without a single real ground." For Iago to tell Othello, "Beware, my lord, of Jealousy" does not prove Desdemona guilty, but is "much better: it is an absolute block to any possible proof of her innocence." Lewis's illustration is far from clear, but his general line of argument is that to assume Ahriman's existence, then interpret every expression of doubt as Ahriman's manipulation of one's opponent is to be caught in a trap of one's own setting, one that compels the dupe to suppress "every struggle of the wounded, but not dead reason" to escape.[8] Still Ulsterman enough to be very anti-Catholic,[9] Lewis instances the warnings given Roman Catholics to treat every doubt as a satanic temptation. A reader of the *Screwtape Letters* who reflects upon the disturbing parallel between the supposed activities of Ahriman and those of Wormwood must wonder how far by 1942 Lewis himself had become a "bulverist."

Lewis's final criticism of Steinerian mental training at this juncture, the rejection of intuition as a ground of belief, brings up an important principle.

45

If what most people call the "real world" is a construction from sense-experience, "one sense confirming another, details supplied by memory and imagination, theory, hypothesis," and if a sense-intuition not fitting into that construction is "scrapped and called an 'illusion,'" then no isolated experience can carry conviction. Only in so far as experiences "fit together into a growing wholeness" can they "make up what we call the real...." Barfield certainly took this point, for the wholeness that must confirm sense-experience became a cardinal assumption in *De Toto et Parte* and his subsequent books.

CHAPTER 4

Assault on Anthroposophy

The *Summa* is the most difficult and curious piece of prose Lewis ever wrote. Its close-knit ratiocination makes it virtually incomprehensible as a whole. Especially baffling are the first three sections of Book I, in which Lewis tries by *reductio ad absurdum* to show how inconceivable he finds the anthroposophical doctrine concerning etheric and astral bodies exploring spiritual worlds. The *Summa*'s strangeness results from its combination of dense, complex argument with sometimes naïve drawing of hard-and-fast distinctions and an old-world lecture-room air given off by its very title, *Clivi Hamiltonis Summae Metaphysices Contra Anthroposophos Libri II*. Evidently its learned young author pored over leather-bound volumes in Duke Humphrey's Library as excitedly as his scientific contemporaries sought to split the atom at Cambridge.

Lewis modelled it upon the medieval academic disputation, specifically Aquinas' *Summa contra Gentiles*. He wrote it in a notebook supplied by Barfield, who in jest describes it as "the joint product of C.S.L. and myself in our youth." In view of Barfield's fierce criticisms of this "joint product," he can only be alluding to the notebook and perhaps the medieval custom by which the tutor wrote a stylised treatise based upon a disputation by his students.[1] Within the two books, I: *Being* and II: *Value*, Lewis sets out his arguments under 21 and 25 headings respectively.

Since Lewis could not long persist in destructive criticism, he soon turned to expounding his own current ideas compounded of Platonism, Manicheism, tragic Stoicism and Christianity. As it stood, the *Summa* must have appeared too densely-argued, in places too arid, for publication unless heavily revised. In any case, Lewis would soon have needed to revise its content to accommodate his orthodox-Christian beliefs.

Nevertheless, the treatise is indispensable for any student wishing to trace the development of Lewis's values, psychology and style of argument. He arranged human spiritual activities in a hierarchy owing much to the medieval designs representing the *trivium* and *quadrivium* hierarchically, with Philosophy at the apex.[2] As already mentioned, Lewis's hierarchy also owes much to Croce's then fashionable *Philosophy of the Spirit*. He developed Alexander's distinction between the Contemplated and the

Enjoyed, and, most fruitfully of all, constructed some of those striking and elaborate analogies for which he is renowned as a stylist. Indeed his whole argument in the *Summa*, so far as it hangs together at all, depends upon the ancient Christian analogy between divine Creation and authorship that he was to use so effectively in his religious books.

As we have seen, Lewis intended to discredit anthroposophical teaching in the eyes of Barfield because of its authoritarian and "bulverist," even paranoiac tendencies, because its identification of imagination with truth would for him have destroyed the unique value of myth, legend, epic and lyric poem,[3] and because he distrusted the practice of self-contemplation. Initially the reader finds himself all at sea owing to the odd, indirect method of dissuasion, that leaves him uncertain when the author is indulging in solemn pastiche and when expressing genuine convictions. The difficulty is, if anything, compounded by the notes Lewis scrawled in red pencil upon borrowing back the manuscript some years later.[4] Just when he seems to have written tongue-in-cheek, his tick or scrawled "Concedo" will indicate continued conviction, and by a remark apparently characteristic of the mature Lewis, his "Nego" or barely decipherable caveat will raise doubts.

Primarily, in the opening sections, Lewis opposes the Steinerian belief in "supersensible" worlds inhabited by spiritual beings and accessible to human souls. His own ambivalence makes the first three sections especially difficult to follow. On the one hand, he pretends to prove the world, even other bodies and souls, a mere mental construct, in order to ridicule Barfield's Coleridgean idealism; on the other hand Lewis assumes with Kant that things-in-themselves are unknowable and therefore that the subject can know any external object only as an image or representation in his own mind. As ironist, Lewis affirms with mock gravity that since his neighbour appears by words and a "mere brute coincidence" of events to share the same "material world," he must assume the material world in his neighbour's soul to be a replica of that in his own, so that there must be as many independent worlds as there are souls. "My neighbour cannot lift the arm of what *I* call 'his' body, but when he lifts the arm of what *he* calls 'his' body ... the similar body moves its arm in mine."

As philosopher, Lewis asserts his own dualism against his opponent's monism by means of a paradox. The mind's perceptions, though dependent on experience in a material world, and transmitted by nerve-impulses, are themselves immaterial. Because the mind has a history, presupposing time, and a propensity to err, presupposing some external source of truth, it "cannot be conceived apart from its world, and is indeed included in that world: but that world itself is included in my mind. Therefore my mind is included in my mind." Lewis escapes from this circle by defining the mind that is included as "myself," limited in space and time, and the mind that includes as "Spirit," "what I really am." The individual soul's life therefore becomes a mere episode in that of the universal creative Spirit, conflicts between its will and Spirit being but apparent.

Having read and first aspired to teach Philosophy, Lewis knew the term "Spirit" as employed by Bradley for "God," by Hegel for both the divine creative power and the historical process, and by Croce for the creative tendency (Alexander's "nisus") within history.[5] As a tutor in English literature and regular reader of "The Prelude," Lewis knew and by his description of "Spirit" recalled Wordsworth's "mighty Mind." Spirit is "pure Subject, enjoyed but never contemplated," without beginning, limit or cause, "eternal, free and infinite." Since we can only "enjoy" and never externally observe Spirit, we cannot project into it qualities we observe in other souls, such as purpose, love or moral attributes.

On this basis, Lewis denies the anthroposophical assertion that the soul can either know spiritual beings from other worlds or, in X-ray fashion, read other souls in this one. Since the soul enjoys itself, it can only contemplate itself as correlative of other souls or external objects. Therefore "I as Spirit create my soul and the environment in which it has meaning by one and the same act." If souls could enjoy each other, they would "lapse into Spirit" and become one. The soul, therefore, can only observe another soul, but "a soul contemplated is exactly what we mean by a body . . . the talking, loveable or detestable, transparent body of our neighbour *in concreto*." The "compresence of souls" and the need to distinguish the inner life each enjoys from the appearance contemplated by the other souls necessitates "some sort of material world."[6] This demands a duality of body and soul, for even the occultist can claim no more than the ability to read a soul from its "aura" or shadowy body. Having no meaning out of its material context, the soul can never leave the body in trance or sleep. Here Lewis apparently misunderstands Steiner, whose assertion that the "astral body" and "Ego" leave the sleeping "etheric" and physical bodies implies no more than that the sleeper feels and perceives realities and events indiscernible by the senses.[7]

The analogies, mainly literary, in which Lewis dismisses any possibility of acquaintance with supposed spiritual "intermediaries" between individual souls and Spirit deserve detailed discussion. If Shakespeare be Hamlet's "intermediary," the Prince can enjoy Shakespeare as long as Shakespeare wills, but can never contemplate him nor know other intermediaries (Ben Jonson, for example), nor their *dramatis personae*. Hamlet in turn acts as intermediary between Shakespeare and the Player-King, who can enjoy but

49

not contemplate Hamlet, while the Prince can contemplate but not enjoy characters on his own level, such as Polonius.

Here Lewis implies a hierarchy ascending from characters in the "Murder of Gonzago" through characters in the Danish court, through Shakespeare as "intermediary" sustaining all his characters, to Spirit as source of every being, real or fictional. In another elaborate analogy, Lewis epitomises his hierarchical system. "Every leaf on the tree is in uninterrupted connection with the next leaf until you go back to the common spray, at which neither leaf exists." Sprays and branches have no inter-connection, for "there is no passage *across*" between worlds, "only ascent to the level before the bifurcation." The soul cannot ascend to any such higher level without surrendering its separate existence, for it and its world "are correlatives and the soul does not mean anything out of its world."

Spirit creates or annihilates souls as an author his characters. Should Shakespeare so much as stare out of the window, Hamlet for that interval ceases to exist, and when Shakespeare resumes his "Hamlet-consciousness" the Prince can know nothing of events during Shakespeare's fit of abstraction. If for a million years the soul ceased to enjoy Spirit, it would remember no interval. (Here Lewis's parallel is dubious, for the soul would note changes in the world.)

Despite being the only begetter of his characters, Shakespeare can deny a measure of freedom only to the minor ones. Iago's creation, for example, represents the successful escape of "the Iago-element in Shakespeare." Similarly, the soul becomes "what she wills to be" by maintaining her separation from Spirit. This free-choice, Lewis adds, "would in theology be called divine justice."[8] Since the soul thus creates herself, she cannot be created, or even manipulated, by beings from any other world.

Lewis ridicules the notion of souls leaving entranced bodies to explore higher worlds. As the dying Hamlet is assimilated into the richness of Shakespeare, so at death the soul lapses into Spirit, wherein it may be "eternal and blessed and truly living" provided "it will consent to die." Mystics reporting other-worldly experiences are guilty of absurd "fictions" tantamount to saying they had been "out of time for a time." Those "other worlds" described in "popular mythologies" must be "distant regions" within our space-time system, or we could not reach them "after" death. Each existing description either "removes them from phenomenal conditions" so as to render meaningless the soul's survival, or attributes to them material or quasi-material conditions, as in "doctrines of the subtle or etheric body."

Conversely, Lewis ridicules that cardinal Christian belief, the Incarnation, by means of the very comparison he later used in expounding it, for he says it makes no more sense than to expect a dramatist to walk into his own play. Eternity, he concludes, can be realised neither by journeying to other worlds nor by supposing God to have journeyed to this, but only "dying into Spirit."[9]

No less sternly, Lewis condemns Steiner's proposed cultivation of self-consciousness. The soul attains its *summum bonum* through self-negation, and we become spiritual through "turning our eyes outward" rather than inward. We should strive "not to contemplate our own souls" but to "enjoy Spirit . . . by contemplating the world, in art, philosophy, history or imagination." Souls that seek Spirit within themselves incur the dangers of "great reactions (the dark night of the soul)," or the "great folly" of "ascetic practices . . . verging on perversion," or the "great wickedness" of "antinomianism," becoming laws unto themselves. The touchstone of any spiritual activity is whether, like Spirit, it "looks outward and hastens . . . to embody itself in matter."

What Lewis says here has very broad implications. Whether consciously or not, he allies himself with a considerable phalanx of twentieth-century authors who for one reason or another regard artistic creation as a struggle to attain detachment and impersonality: Yeats, Eliot, Lawrence, Hemingway, to name four who have little else in common. The statement implies also that the best criticism should consider not the artist but the artefact, as Lewis memorably maintained in his controversy with E. M. W. Tillyard.[10] More broadly still, it implies a condemnation not necessarily of psycho-analysis practised clinically, but of the whole tradition of self-analysis and self-concern that has spawned the innumerable therapies in vogue today. But this condemnation logically implies faith in duty and the "rightness" of the natural order, a faith more consistent with Lewis's later orthodox theism than his current pantheism. Within a mere three or four years, he was to work out his transition from implicit to explicit Christian faith in *The Pilgrim's Regress*.

Lewis's statement, moreover, implies dissent from the "metaphysical" and Byronic varieties of Romanticism, respectively self-analytical and antinomian. Nor could Lewis entertain the post-romantic belief in a "coming of age" that would enable man to live by moral intuition rather than external commandment. Still less could he credit Steiner's assumption that knowledge was attainable by meditation rather than study of facts or documents.

In a sense, Lewis's complex argument against anthroposophical ethics in Book II depends upon a misinterpretation. When Steiner claimed that a free human spirit need obey no external commandment, he defined freedom not as unbridled license but as the fully self-conscious soul's capacity for intelligent decision.[11] The free spirit would, for example, understand why citizens were required to obey traffic regulations or pay taxes and so keep the laws concerned with informed assent rather than blind adherence. Socrates acted as a free spirit in choosing to die under the law rather than be smuggled out of Athens.

Lewis's argument runs as follows. Since creation of souls necessitates creation of "resistant matter" (a point made in *The Problem of Pain* to justify suffering), pleasure or pain must result from the coincidence or conflict between matter and the soul's momentary will. Under stress of the consequent passion, the perceptions must be limited, or even corrupted. Only by a victorious struggle, therefore, can human souls fulfil their collective function of multiplying consciousness so that their diversity and even their limitations "add richness to the life of Spirit." To see objects as they are, "as Spirit sees them," involves an effort and strain symbolised in the doctrine of the Fall. Lewis cannot therefore regard obedience to moral authority as unspiritual: "The first stage" of spiritual enlightenment is "to will rightly," the second to view "the law of right willing—which appears at first as an arbitrary and external command—" as being "what I at my deepest level really will, as opposed to my trivial and rebellious moods."

How so rigorous a moralist could, later in Book II, indict religion as "the great enemy of the spiritual life" becomes clear only in the light of his ascending hierarchy of the modes of spiritual experience. This, as will be remembered, was based on Croce's postulate of a "spirit of history" implicit in events and successively expressed in artistic and logical modes, in ethics and final historiography. Because Croce viewed History as having no origin, meaning or purpose beyond itself, he rejected all religious or metaphysical explanations.

Lewis divides the spiritual life into practical and theoretical modes. The practical mode is Morality, "willing as Spirit wills." In a sound ethic, "such as was propounded by Kant," Spirit would be the sole absolute and Morality not intrinsically superior to other modes of spiritual life but pre-emptive because concerned with action, which "articulates and commands our whole life" since "only by doing . . . or refusing to do something" can we "meet or shun any other experience." Lewis elsewhere remarks that we abandon pursuit of another absolute, for example Beauty, if "an interrupting duty knocks at our door." He never abandoned this puritan stress upon conduct, traceable in English authors from Fielding and Johnson to Jane Austen, Arnold and George Eliot. His phrase "willing as Spirit wills" does not imply blind obedience to commandments, however, but rather Kant's Categorical Imperative, willing the action any person should take, for the notion of "Spirit" includes that of a cosmic will or conscience. While unable to accept Barfield's anthroposophical belief in the identity of thought practised by various minds contemplating the same idea, Lewis did always believe in a common core of morality within different religious or social systems, what he later called "The Tao."

Of the theoretical modes of spiritual experience, Science ranks lowest, originating, in Lewis's view, in a power-wish and consisting of primarily subjective abstractions from reality. Next comes History (including Natural History), whose objects, being less abstract, are viewed more "as Spirit sees." Above History Lewis, unlike Croce, ranks Art. Being dispensed from any requirement to treat of subjective or objective material, Art "presents objects to us with the greatest concreteness." It can be even more concrete than History, even more systematic than Science, for "we understand all the reciprocal relations within a play or story more fully than Science can ever understand the world." Art, however, can offer no more than a "foretaste or shadow of the full consciousness of Spirit" since its objects may be "subjective fancies." Art trains us in disinterestedness, hence is "propaedeutic" to the spiritual life. Again, Lewis enunciates a conviction he always held. Presumably he ranks "Science" below "Natural History" because he has in mind a mathematical discipline (Croce's "Logical mode") rather than an inductive one.

Philosophy transcends the foregoing theoretical modes by enabling us to know "that we are Spirit and will the objects that seem to condition us." This knowledge, however, cannot constitute that "immediately conscious participation" in Spirit Lewis considers the highest mode of spiritual life, for such a mode would be essentially moral and emotional rather than intellectual. In the state of Charity, the soul not only sees others as they really are ("as Spirit sees them") but in disinterested benignity wills their continuance. Lewis, foreshadowing his permanent beneficence to individuals rather than causes, considers that Charity can extend only to neighbouring souls.

The completely spiritual mode of experience must have the universality of Science, the concreteness of History, the disinterestedness of Art; it must also like Philosophy be free from "the great primary abstraction" and like Charity be consciously co-operative with Spirit. (What Lewis meant by the "primary abstraction" must be considered later.) Souls enjoying this supreme experience have become "as clear glasses for Spirit to see through," able to take their sufferings "as we now take the tragedies of the poets, where pain and wickedness . . . only contribute to the goodness of the whole." Lewis finds this detachment intermittently practised in Memory but fully established in Imagination, a universal empathy permitting transcendental vision of all objects and creatures as manifestations of Spirit even if, like slums or cancer, they are accounted evils. The soul so blessed feels nowhere alienated and everywhere at home.

In what Barfield called a "noble passage," Lewis portrays this supreme spiritual state as an apparent re-discovery after "long exile" inasmuch as "we . . . recognise that we are Spirit and are everywhere in our own country and our own house." It appears both as "longing" and "fruition," a "losing" yet also a "keeping," because we sense our "dual nature" and self-division, as "Spirit that possesses all" and soul abandoning all. "To others," Lewis continues, echoing Wordsworth, we shall appear to "have fallings from us and vanishings, as though the world has become a "prospect in the mind," for to the human limit we shall have become "pure Spirit." Alternatively, we shall appear to love the object only "because we are its creator and will it into being." Other imaginative souls will experience "dead things" as "charged with life" and imbue with "vague personality" the very hills and trees, that "share the life of Spirit, which knows itself alive beneath its vesture." Such moments, Lewis avers, are our "highest life" for "their continuation would be the redemption of the world." Clearly he envisages "this highest form of the spiritual life . . . Imagination" as a prolongation of experiences often described as mystical illuminations, "spots of time," "epiphanies" or the moments of insight known to philosophers and scientists.

Since Imagination, as Lewis describes it, fuses together moral, mystical, aesthetic and cognitive forms of illumination, how can it fail to be in essence religious? Good to him resides not in the object but in the way we perceive it. Our bond with Spirit, though subjective, can be strengthened by deliberate extraversion. Because Spirit "first disenchants and then re-enchants the world,"[12] the idolatrous effort to repeat a spiritual experience mistakenly attributed to its attendant circumstances will reveal its true source. Religion, being compounded of this "idolatry" and unreliable assertions of fact, is "inimical to the spiritual life."

Lewis soon hedges his indictment about with so many qualifications as to betray his emotional unease. Religion, for example, might involve Charity and Morality, but these are no whit less spiritual for being practised without accompanying illusions. Indeed, Morality practised in deference to a god's "supposed commandment" ceases to be spiritual. Lewis may have felt that this undercut his earlier defence of obedience to moral law, for his indictment of religion ends in partial withdrawal: "Religion, at its best, may be described as the whole spiritual life with accompanying confusions of thought."

The spiritual life, as Lewis sees it, culminates in imagination, which converts any "first-degree" mode of spiritual experience—art, history or science—into one of the "second degree," ranking, for example, with charity or morality. This implies that the infusion of imagination into any other intellectual activity raises that activity to a higher order. Again Lewis qualifies his assertion, saying that the complete spiritual life involves viewing all events, including "our own sufferings," as we would "events in a tragedy," and that since this constitutes the supreme fortitude, we can "treat morality as the whole spiritual life." Once again he accords a special priority to moral good.

Because "History, Memory, Science, etc." only attain their full spiritual value if touched with imagination, to regard a myth or symbol as factually true would amount to "idolatry," by which Lewis means the attribution of absolute value to whatever has contingent value as a focus for imagination, "the activity of discerning as Spirit." Imagination neither needs nor admits of justification, for the word "*because* ... presupposes that reasons *outside* the spiritual could commend it ... and absolue value cannot be sanctioned by empirical value."

After avowing "concern about my own spiritual experience" to be no part of the spiritual life, Lewis concludes his *Summa contra Anthroposophos* in such an outpouring of *contemptus mundi* as would have chilled and delighted the heart of any ancient Stoic or Manichee:

> Since the contempt of worldly values is a preliminary to the spiritual life, souls are in danger if they think too much about those objects whose worldly value is too great for their present strength. All thinking about health or riches, or about happiness, or the possible survival of the soul after death, or about God or the gods, or demons, is to be counted dangerous, as we count it dangerous to dwell on topics that inflame our passions in grosser, though it may be less fatal, ways.

Much interesting discussion of literary genres and values has had to be deferred for later consideration. While Lewis's concept of imagination has some features that remained permanent—*Senhsucht*, the delight that is also unbearable belonging, for example—the concluding passage just quoted betrays an immature striking of an old-world moral posture that, fortunately, he soon outgrew. The young Lewis appears to detect no inconsistency between attributing supreme importance to the way he views phenomena and denying any value to self-awareness. While his lifelong preference for extraversion needs no defence, it is difficult to see how one can consciously lead the spiritual life if forbidden to enquire whether one is doing so. For all his modern sources of argumentation, the author of *Summa* might be a schoolman spinning fine webs of reasoning without regard to total impression or daily experience.

CHAPTER 5

Defence and Counter-Attack

Barfield's rejoinders, both his critical notes headed *Replicit Anthroposophus Barfieldus* and his more general reflections headed *Autem,* strike one as products of a mind less organised than Lewis's but more attuned to reality. To speak frankly, he often seems more grown-up. Though unable to match his opponent's dialectical figure-skating, rhythmic phrasing and gift for analogy, he shrewdly exposes contradictions in terms and misuse of language, and eventually feels his way towards undiscovered country. However memorably phrased, much argumentation in the *Summa* emanates from a young don, a trained intellect of, at times, facile brilliance, whereas *Replicit* and, still more, *Autem* reveal a creative mind becoming.

Barfield's greater maturity can be illustrated from two criticisms in *Replicit.* First, he objects to Lewis's "spiritual" consideration of affliction: "What troubles me here is that, if I elected to dedicate my life to the *increasing* of slum tenements and cancers, that too would be 'part of the world which would be found valuable if we saw spiritually'." (Lewis could have said this in half the space, but Barfield realised it had to be said.) Secondly, to Lewis's refusal to concern himself over his own spiritual progress, Barfield objects shrewdly: "Whatever the dangers of self-observation, a refusal to face them constitutes an 'egoism of caution'." Here Barfield hit upon a self-protective rejection of emotional complexity that Lewis never quite outgrew.

Barfield falls upon some errors and contradictions in the *Summa.* First, he points out that if souls are to be "as clear glass for Spirit to shine through" they cannot also "multiply consciousness" by supplying diverse viewpoints. Secondly, souls cannot *be* Spirit yet also co-operate *with* Spirit. Thirdly, showing a certain mordant wit, Barfield explodes an unfortunate analogy depicting the soul's relationship to Spirit as that of a man positioned between a lantern and a white wall, whose shadow supposedly grows smaller and more distinct as he retreats from the wall. Pointing out that the opposite would happen, Barfield comments: "Analogies drawn from light would appear to be especially dangerous to those who are fanatically determined to keep their backs to it."

Barfield voices four more general complaints about the *Summa*. His first, that to describe the soul as "cause of the body's behaviour" is to misuse words, initiates a discussion bringing out a fundamental conflict. Barfield, as a monist, argues that a man's body and behaviour constitute his soul's "expression and imagination," since imagination "projects meaning into space" as speech does into sound. In *Replies to Objections*, Lewis responds by defining the body as "the soul contemplated" and the soul as "the power . . . active in the human body." This, he adds, presupposes within any human being an active and a passive element. Here Lewis expounds the Cartesian dualism he always maintained, while Barfield's monism seems an embryonic expression of a now fashionable assumption evident in the phrase "body language." As will be shown later, Barfield worked out the implications of a monistic psychology in a complicated diagram.

Secondly, Barfield denounces Lewis's "Box-and-Cox" alternation between contemplation and enjoyment. He argues that the very meaning of imagination, considered as a term in aesthetic or social discourse, is "that which raises the contemplator . . . to a participation in enjoyment." What the imaginative observer enjoys is not "the other soul herself" but "the same that she enjoys." By reason of this "*sympathein*" between the observer's mind and another's, the other person's body acquires a "transparency" to the observer. Pushing his argument further, Barfield suggests on "good evidence," even perhaps "the warrant of our own experience," that another person need not be physically present for "compresence[1] and intercourse of soul with soul" to occur. He does not say what intuitions he in London and Lewis in Oxford had experienced about each other's thoughts, nor how they affect his monistic concept of body and soul.

Instead, Barfield compares poetic and "occult" awareness. Both involve an ascent from contemplation to "con-enjoyment" and ultimately to viewing all things in their cosmic context, as enjoined in the *Summa*. What a poet merely senses, an occultist consciously expresses in "a system of established metaphors," for example colours denoting qualities in bodies or objects.[2] Because the occultist has earned his knowledge and spiritual freedom by fulfilling "hard conditions," overcoming egotism and becoming indifferent to "success," he utters not mere fancy but "the truth of the spirit."

Barfield's third objection proved difficult for his opponent to follow. In the *Hamlet* analogy, he suggests, resides a concealed assumption, that Hamlet's soul is a single entity. Rather, Barfield argues, we should view the soul of Hamlet, or anyone else, as a "manifold of instincts and passions," each conceivably enjoyed by "a different intermediary." Barfield agrees on the aim

57

of philosophy as being "intellectual penetration to the One" but denies that a human being is one save "at the level at which Beaumont and Fletcher are one." A human being does not inherit oneness but attains it by learning to "contemplate, and so objectify" his intermediaries. Lewis replied that human passions, often conflicting, were conceivable only in relation to their objects, which were to be found within a totality necessarily contained in the mind of some single intermediary between the soul and Spirit. In Lewis's view, two minds cannot share the same "*phantasia.*" This reply evidently failed to satisfy Barfield, who scrawled a violent but incomprehensible marginal note "My God! what about *Summa* I with (i)."

Barfield clarifies his objection in a long addendum to his criticism of the *Hamlet* analogy. "Intermediaries," he asserts, are not convenient fictions but actual entities whose existence the soul must realise before it can attain its full potential. As it passes from the unknowing enjoyment to the contemplation of these intermediaries, so will his reader's self-consciousness expand, with resultant "worship and thankfulness before the Beings who have been keeping such a treasure laid up for you in heaven." Barfield compares this expansion of spiritual awareness with the process by which people pass from hero worshipping great minds as "veritable intermediaries" to contemplating them as mere exemplars. Ferdinand can only approach Shakespeare through Prospero, whom he first experiences as his "very destiny," but having encountered Shakespeare Ferdinand still loves but now contemplates Prospero rather than seeing the world through Prospero's eyes.

In his *Replies to Objections*, Lewis refuses to go beyond agreeing that abler human beings could transmit spiritual insight. Although he came to believe in angels, he ascribed tutelary functions only to comparable beings in his space-fantasies, for example the Oyarsa in *Perelandra*. Influenced by Barfield's contention, in *Replicit*, that the average man enjoyed Spirit in feelings rather than thoughts, Lewis did eventually believe that the common man or the child could attain the divine vision. Significantly, however, (like Shakespeare) Lewis best disclosed his vision of redeemed nature and humanity in his young characters. Spiritual illumination, the vision of human and external regenerate, carries far more conviction in the child-characters of *The Lion, the Witch and the Wardrobe* than in the banal adult figures of *That Hideous Strength*.

Fourthly, Barfield objects to Lewis's claim that proof of a mythic being's actual existence would deprive that being of symbolic value. This, to Barfield, contradicts an assertion made earlier in the *Summa*, that in Imagination Spirit knows itself alive under a natural vesture that therefore becomes symbolic.

Brushing aside Lewis's counter-argument that a symbol is not something given but something taken by "free spiritual activity," Barfield retorts that if Imagination is "taking" the symbol, then the symbol is "taken" by Spirit —and therefore also "given."

In his further reflections headed *Autem*, Barfield more radically criticises the *Summa*. For Lewis, he says, making distinctions has become an end in itself. Moreover, the tractate's "very structure of thought . . . is inadequate to the subject." An intellectual system based on simplistic axioms like "A is either A or not-A" pertains to a static world. A "knowing" to which "this proposition is made the *scaffold*"[3] rather than one tool of thought among many is adequate only to the "mineral world in a state of repose," and quite inadequate for discussion of matters "abstract, aesthetic, spiritual"—an allusion, perhaps, to Steiner's "Saturn-era" that saw the formation of mineral matter and the physical body. Barfield continues, "Other metaphors are required here than the concealed mineral metaphor known as logic."[4] Even a living plant at any given moment "both *is* and *is not* any given shape, height, etc.," *a fortiori* the animal or human soul. Furthermore, in the very act of describing Imagination as making us aware of our "dual nature" as "the Spirit that possesses all and the soul that is abandoning that possession" Lewis, says Barfield, is implying a state of simultaneous enjoyment and contemplation.

Barfield's charge drew a characteristic Lewisian rebuttal. Lewis defends the "Law of Contradiction" as a fundamental principle rather than the temporarily convenient hypothesis properly described as a "scaffold." A law that can be disregarded at will is no law. On this law even Barfield's argument depends, for supposing (i) a vegetable "is and is not" a given size, (ii) that statement is self-contradictory, but if (iii) both it and the law of contradiction be true, the two "truths" are mutually contradictory. Since (iv) two truths cannot be in contradiction, then (v) the law of contradiction is untrue. But in that case, Barfield's whole argument, which involves principle (iv), is invalid. All that the vegetable example shows is that to apply the concept of Being where that of Becoming is requisite produces contradiction just because "what is contradictory when approached with the wrong concepts may prove coherent when we have hit on the right concepts."

In the short term, the *Note on the Law of Contradiction* convinced Barfield, who applied this principle in *De Toto et Parte* and expounded it himself in *Romanticism Comes of Age*. In a later essay, however, he argues that the law of logical exclusion, far from being a law of nature, is a manifestation of a "parochial interlude' 'in the history of philosophy.[5] Recently he has remarked: "The cogency of Lewis's arguments was very important to my whole development. To ignore them is to accept mishmash, so I have spent a lifetime on the distinguo: 'Logic, yes; but then logic itself, properly understood, is polar, or it is nothing'."[6]

What Barfield means by "polar logic" may be glimpsed from his criticisms, in *Autem*, of the *Summa*'s allegedly inadequate psychology. Essentially he tries to amend a conception of Spirit and soul that denies value to feeling. According to the *Summa*, inasmuch as Spirit "contemplates," it thinks, and inasmuch as the soul "enjoys," it wills. Between these two states, as between Spirit and soul, an intermediary, in this case Feeling, is needed. Human beings can only communicate with the divine if the divine include Love among its attributes. Lewis's "Charity," the mere willing of another's existence, accomplishes little if unaccompanied by elemental human feeling. Since neither enjoyment and contemplation nor thinking and willing suffice to define metaphysical and psychological relationships, then in each case some third principle must mediate.

The relationship between the three principles can only be envisaged in metaphor:

> Against the principle that "A is either A or not-A" we can set, *for example*, the principle of "polarity" as it is conceived in ... electricity, where two extremes are in one sense opposite and in another sense the same, and where the "state of strain" between these two extremes together with the variously rhythmic variations which it sets up may be expressed as in itself a third principle.

Later Barfield was to claim that "every act of imagination" unites two opposed forces.[7]

Here he adds that "the spiritual austerity of pure will" must be energised by "the human warmth of desire." The soul manifesting Christian chivalric courage (Barfield cites Latin *cor*, "the heart," as root) will actively combat evils that Stoic fortitude passively endures. Again, in love as distinct from willed beneficence, imagination creates sympathy ("feeling-with"). On the metaphysical plane, a contemplative but non-participating Spirit is replaced by a threefold deity that as Father contemplates (thinkingly observes) His creation, as Holy Spirit enjoys (wills from within) human souls, and as Son mediates (compassionately acts).[8]

It would be less than honest to conclude this account of Barfield's reaction to the *Summa* without pointing out his important areas of agreement with Lewis. For the long and eloquent account of Imagination he offers "humble congratulations and thanks." Like Lewis, he believes in a spiritual One that symbolically expresses itself in the Many, i.e. phenomena. Above all, he agrees with Lewis in denying Marxian or Freudian reductiveness, the derivation of human imagination and reason from the "foul rag-and-bone shop" of the appetites. For all their unresolved disagreements, both young scholars believe human existence to have a meaning referrable to man's prospect rather than his origin.

CHAPTER 6

A Dispute on Virtue

In *De Bono et Malo*, Lewis attempts to define good and evil in terms of the soul's relation to Spirit. This theme naturally interested him during his slow conversion from pantheism to Christianity. The tractate gives evidence that its author is nearing his spiritual resting-place not only by its largely Christian ethic but by its allusions: the term "God" used occasionally for "Spirit," the quotations from Christ and St. Paul, the approving citation of the "Christian myth" of the Fall. To the literary reader its main interest lies in its anticipation of Lewis's teaching on evil in his *Preface to "Paradise Lost."* For this reason and because it does not deal with the issues to be explored later in this monograph, *De Bono* warrants full consideration now.

Lewis begins by recalling his statement in the *Summa* that to emerge from Spirit souls needed a common, resistant environment, just as players must observe the rules of a game even to their own inconvenience. He defines the soul's ideal good as the state of being "numerically distinct" from but "qualitatively one" with Spirit. The soul's ultimate evil, he has suggested, is a state of entire separation from Spirit, consequent upon the passions aroused by the soul's conflict with its environment. In the rest of his essay, Lewis poses a series of questions about good and evil and the motives for preferring to do good.

First he asks whether absolute Evil exists, since neither it nor absolute Good is realisable in human experience. Even in principle, Lewis concludes, evil is no more than the total absence of good. In actual life, human beings know only better and worse conduct, more redolent of Spirit or more ego-centric. The soul that has descended from altruism towards egoism prefers whatever makes it "least of a unity." Among physical pleasures it will choose those permitting it to live in "sheerly separate moments of undesired and unrecollected pleasure, over any demanding unity of apperception." The "ideal term" of such conduct would be "mere sensation without self-consciousness," psychological disintegration.

Metaphysically, the evil soul, by ceasing to be self-conscious, has relapsed downward into Spirit. As "Christian myth" bears out, however, absolute evil is a contradiction in terms:

For evil there begins with a being who attempts to become God. But to treat oneself as God means to treat oneself as the whole: and this is precisely what a soul does when it does not go beyond the individual good. For that which needs not to go beyond the individual good is God or Spirit, because his individuality is universality.

Here, a good dozen years before composing his *Preface to "Paradise Lost"*, Lewis gives the gist of his celebrated account of Satan, which he had no doubt already begun to convey in tutorials.

Lewis answers his next question, whether absolute Good can exist, by suggesting that good and evil souls relapse into Spirit in different ways, the good soul remaining "an element in Spirit," the evil soul having "broken up into isolated sensations." The good soul relapses "as a shade of colour loses its individuality" in a painting, the evil soul "as a herb is pounded to make the pigment itself." The one resembles a "subordinate piece of mechanism," the other a "broken machine" scrapped and melted down for use in the manufacture of a new machine. The greatest conceivable good, being a "copy or faint echo of Spirit," reveals its divine origin, whereas the greatest conceivable evil, so far from implying some principle of absolute Chaos, amounts simply to a former wholeness now disintegrated.

Lewis's negative answer is more convincing than his reasoning and imagery. The good soul's loss of individual significance contrasts somewhat with the assertion in the *Summa* that such souls "multiply consciousness" by contributing individual viewpoints to Spirit. The machine images jar with Lewis's individualism and prejudice against technology. The distinction between absolute Chaos and disintegrated wholeness, if logically tenable, needs the genius of Milton for its imaginative realisation.

Playing a variation on an age-old theme, Lewis now enquires how Spirit, "being all, can be good," since it must apparently include whatever evil things exist. He replies that as a colour isolated from a picture may appear ugly, so parts of a good whole can be evil out of their context. A soul, therefore, becomes evil by making itself a self-existent absolute. Without considering practical difficulties, for example the moral quality of the soul forced into isolation, Lewis adds elusively that though all souls contribute to the goodness of Spirit, good souls are so in themselves. Though all souls will *"what* Spirit wills," good souls will *"as* Spirit wills." Here Lewis, it might be objected, is trying to reap the benefits of freewill and determinism at once.

Lewis presents his next question, "Why do right?" in three different forms. First he asks "Why is good good?" He suggests that any answer must be axiomatic, for the good of an action lies either in its end, one known intuitively to be desirable, or else in the "universal good" of duty or the "particular good" of pleasure. He now puts his question in personal terms: "Why ought I to do right?" As in the *Summa*, he answers that even if moral good be but one of many goods, it is "the good of action," so that to say "it is good to do this" means "I ought to do it."[1] This principle applies even to the "duty" to seek Truth or create Beauty, since seeking and creating are actions, hence examples of moral good. The reasoning here seems superficial, for there are many good actions—taking out a diseased appendix, for instance— that not everyone should attempt, while the principle that action, as such, is good has horrifying implications. Again, many artists and scientists regard their callings as self-justifying, while others are motivated by the "particular good" of personal advancement: are the disinterested and the ambitious equally commendable?

The objection is forestalled when Lewis puts his question in a third form: "Since all things equally contribute to the forwarding of God's design, and therefore produce good, why ought I to choose virtuous action instead of vicious: for in either case I shall be producing good?" This time he reaffirms the primacy of motive over frequently uncontrollable consequence, then ponders some implications of his answer. One who to attain some supreme and otherwise unattainable good assumes the role of "devil" in the sense of "tempter" acts rightly. To suggest that he enact the devil's role in the fuller sense of becoming "absolutely evil" is meaningless, since we cannot label an act "diabolic" yet by description show it "virtuous." To illustrate Lewis's distinction, he would presumably approve the act of tempting Hitler to bomb London rather than continue the Battle of Britain, but disapprove that of fire-bombing Dresden. The distinction, however, can apply to but a few of the actions required to wage war, even in a just cause. Neither in *De Bono* nor any of his published writings does Lewis depart from his unshakable Kantian belief that good is absolute, not relative, and necessarily concerned with action.

Lewis's complex answer to an alternative question: 'Since I wish ... to be vicious, may I excuse myself on the ground that even thus I shall be forward-ing God's purpose?" raises an issue on which he and Barfield continue to disagree. Lewis suggests that successive events may appear simultaneous in Spirit's purview (*sub specie aeternitatis*) and so evil actions may form part of the "many-coloured glass" or the divine plan. Lewis adds a caveat, that it is important to realise the limitations of "the symbol that interprets the ever-present perfection of Spirit as the gradual performance by God of a good purpose in time." Above this Barfield notes on the manuscript "Evolution." Because a picture's beauty cannot depend on the order in which we perceive its parts, Lewis argues, it does not follow from Spirit's

ever-present goodness "that 'God' is bringing the world from 'ill' to 'good'."
The notion of eternity he differentiates from that of good produced in time,
citing Von Hügel on the human horror of endless succession, as distinct from
the rapturous apprehension of the eternal.[2] Lewis now renews his attack on
the "popular and exoteric" anthroposophical doctrine of a "god producing
good in time." On that popular level, since the "highest accuracy" rarely
coincides with the "greatest felt reality," the goodness of Spirit has to be
represented in "mythical accounts of the love and goodness of god" and of
divine omnipotence.[3]

This first statement of Lewis's disbelief in progress and in historical
determinism shows that he had as yet attained neither Christian belief nor
Christian humility. As Barfield points out in his essay on "C. S. Lewis and
Historicism," complete scepticism about progress is inconsistent with the
Christian belief in progressive revelation. At this point in his career, Lewis
was too cloistered a don to illustrate his case from the sophistries currently
employed by Marxists and their sympathisers to justify the atrocities
intended to expedite the process of "history" in the U.S.S.R. Nor had he
formed any conviction regarding the application of religious principles to the
social structure. Later he was to find social democracy the most Christian
form of society.[4]

In *De Bono et Malo*, Lewis can understand the contribution of evil to
Spirit only on the "metaphysical" plane. On the "mythical" level, "where
'God' is in time, He may have real enemies" through granting freewill. Since
these evil souls manifest Spirit, a "god" who brings about absolute "good"
in time is inconceivable. We can choose good for ourselves by willing "what
Spirit wills," but can only blunder into evil while seeking "our private good."

Finally, Lewis considers an objection to this ethic: that "a man may make
both yielding and repentance too easy by reflecting that his action will in any
case 'produce good'." This, he points out, arises from the "false philosophy"
that judges actions by their consequences. After alluding to the "true
doctrine" expounded by Kant and in the *Bhaghavad-gita*,[5] he indulges in
one of several Johnsonesque utterances:

> That our wickedness cannot soil the universe as it really is will amaze
> those only who thought that our virtue kept it sweet: and it is a false
> conception of wickedness and selfishness which abandons virtue on finding
> that vice is the ruin of the vicious soul and not of the world.

Politicians, business-men, even games-players may act pragmatically and
satanists may venerate evil ("the shadow"),[6] Lewis admits, but he grounds
his hope on realising good not in future time but in eternity, and in resolving

to judge an action by its performer's motive. "The good soul," he concludes, "is good simply, the evil evil for itself alone."

The essay reveals Lewis at a most absorbing phase. As he alternately preaches and eschews Christian orthodoxy, he swims upstream with the indirect pulsating motion of a spawning salmon. Whereas eighteenth-century deists formally subscribed to a religion they privately regarded as popular mythology, and nineteenth-century rationalists made public their belief yet practised an austere Christian ethic, Lewis progressed in the opposite direction. A decade earlier he had flung scientific materialism at the pious Greeves like any Huxley or Mill, but in *De Bono et Malo* he approaches Christianity via a Platonism tinged with Stoicism, tolerating popular mythology like an eighteenth-century aristocratic deist. But he also swims against the current (an exercise he always enjoyed) in refusing assent to any notions of historical progress or evolution. In time, his equally obstinate assertion of divine transcendance gave birth to a vigorous neo-orthodox movement, that John Betjeman humorously dubbed "St. C. S. Lewis's Church."[7]

Barfield's lengthy but unfinished tractate *De Toto et Parte* offers an alternative ethic. Its author first exposes an inconsistency in Lewis's argument. If by describing good and evil as "ideal terms . . . not revealed in human experience" Lewis means we cannot think about them, is not the same true of the ideal term "relapse into Spirit"? Yet the *Summa*, objects Barfield, "consists almost entirely of thoughts about relapse into Spirit." (By "think about" Barfield presumably means "imagine.") Good and evil appear both to lead towards "lapse into Spirit," so we have no reason to choose one rather than the other. Somewhat caustically, Barfield charges Lewis with avoiding this absurdity by conceiving the "relapse" as a point never actually reached or else by refining its meaning:

> When we are obliged to speak of "two" relapses . . . a "downward relapse and an upward relapse"; when we have to say in one paragraph "before we reach absolute good, we shall have passed beyond soul life altogether" and in the next that "the good soul remains an element in Spirit"; then the advantage, if not the propriety of using the term "relapse" for the limit of the soul's progress towards both good and evil begins to look very doubtful. Has Spirit a top and a bottom?

This criticism annoyed Lewis. In his brief, hastily-written note *Commentarium in Tractatum De Toto et Parte* he retorts that by calling good and evil "ideal" he "meant precisely that they *could* be thought of." Nor has he ever described Spirit as "merely One," or assumed that the relapse never actually happens. Furthermore, "that all 'refining' is subterfuge is the plain man's case against philosophy. Do you wish to maintain it?" Even more angrily, Lewis responds to Barfield's final taunt—"Has Spirit a top and a bottom?"—that "if you pretend not to understand metaphor, you are, in this particular, *morally* wrong." Cooling after his outburst, Lewis explains that the entity "Spirit" comprises both the sub-logical or animal awareness and the supra-logical or mystical insight.

Barfield bases his own doctrine of moral good on two premises, his immediate awareness of being "one self . . . subject of many experiences" and his feeling at least partially free to determine whether the self or the experiences shall predominate. Some experiences, such as sleep, terror or temptation, suspend his self-awareness; others, such as friendship, do not. Up to a point he can decide whether the self shall be one or many, "integrated or disintegrated."[8] Since the self needs something to integrate, the increase of self-consciousness depends on the increase and broadening of experience. Barfield therefore proposes "more integrated" as a synonym for "better" and "integrity" as the essence of "virtue." In the half-century since he wrote *De Toto*, this terminology, and the ethical judgment it expresses, have become commonplace.

From his two premises Barfield argues that in his initial, 'naïve' stage of awareness, "the sum" of his experiences "took the form of a cosmos, or whole consisting of parts." Then he came to realise, "by reflection on the difference between feeling and thought," that " 'I', while remaining one of the parts, must also be *in some sense* the Whole." He cannot therefore accept Lewis's assertion that the soul's destiny is to merge into the cosmic Whole. Self-consciousness, "integrity as I know it," demands an interplay between being a whole and being a part. Spirit, the supreme Good, must therefore denote the limit of integration, heightened rather than diminished self-consciousness. To realise the cosmic Whole as a form is to realise one's own form, and involves not the separation of thought and feeling—contemplation and enjoyment—but their union.

In his *Commentarium*, Lewis answers this romantic assertion by denying that consciousness can be equated with a single self enjoying many experiences, for consciousness "plainly" results from reflection. Moreover he doubts the propriety of lumping together sleep, terror and temptations as interrupters of self-consciousness. Do sleep and intoxication suspend selfhood in the same sense? Sleep and anaesthesia, Lewis suggests, cause the self to "fall apart into atoms of sensation" and so lose its "unity of apperception." There may be various sensations but "no 'I' feeling this pain along with that pain." Sensuality suspends selfhood in a quite different way, for consciousness remains while will disintegrates. The patient under sedation moves towards the "*zero* of self," the drunkard or sensualist towards "dual personality." To stay awake is to "resolve that Barfield shall be one rather than none": to resist temptation is to "resolve that he shall be one rather than many."

Regarding self-consciousness in the lover, Lewis—a bachelor writing to a happily-married friend—admits to some uncertainty. While the lover's state in no way resembles terror or intoxication, it might resemble sleep to the extent of diminishing "the sense 'here am I!'" But, concludes Lewis, "I am vague about all this." Whether Barfield ever challenged him on the distinction between sensuality and love has yet to be revealed.

The remainder of Barfield's argument cannot be grasped without some understanding of the general structure of *De Toto*. The tractate's nine sections deal respectively with: (1) Flaws in Lewis's view of good, evil and "relapse into Spirit"; (2) Self-consciousness; (3) Conceptions of whole and part; (4) Moral integrity involving interplay of "wholeness" and "partness"; (5) The meaning of "being"; (6) The meaning of "Spirit" as supreme Good; (7) The cosmos reflected in its parts, hence its realisation as form necessitating realisation of oneself as form; (8) A list of twelve proposed definitions of terms; (9) Six of those definitions.

In his "Theoria" outlined in (8), Barfield intended to progress in a "closed circle" from the cosmos as "the whole that I can think about" to Spirit, "a part being the whole." He actually provided only six of the twelve intended definitions: I *Cosmos*; II *Thinking* ("the whole being"); III *Feeling* ("a part being"); IV *Will* ("which sunders part from whole and from other parts"); V *Self-consciousness* ("The sundering"); VI *Form* ("The whole being a part.")[9]

Barfield's conclusions about good and evil come in his fourth definition, *Will*. To maintain or increase self-consciousness, the soul must will. Since no will-power is needed to be the Whole, for everything is so by nature, Will is "that which makes me a part" and can therefore only be attributed to the part. It is "dysemplastic," producing the Many from the One which simply "is" (Greek: *to on*). As a thing acts or suffers action, it is a part, requiring another and reciprocating part. Thus "partness and action are inseparable concepts."

By-passing for the present Barfield's assertion that will results from the action of tutelary "intermediaries," we pass to his conception of good. "Virtue is my integrity. Therefore, inasmuch as it is *action*, virtue is the sundering by me of part (myself) from the Whole," hence from other parts. "But inasmuch as it is a *state*, Virtue is the realisation of all these parts as One Whole." Since this realisation cannot be brought about by an act of will, it proceeds from grace, for "it is my duty to be a part and my privilege to discover that I am the Whole. Ethically such a discovery... is grace;

cognitively it is revelation. All genuine art is revelation and all genuine religion the result of it."

Though eloquently phrased, Barfield's statement is open to question, particularly on the difference between good and evil forms of "sundering." Its author, like Lewis, was moving towards his lifelong convictions. Insistence upon self-realisation has among post-romantic moralists, particularly existentialists, replaced the old ethic of self-denial. The paradox that one must be oneself yet apprehend the divine and desire its oversight is woven into anthroposophical teaching. Self-consciousness, the developed Ego, marks the furthest limit of spiritual evolution, according to Steiner, yet that very spiritual maturity proceeds from the outgrowing of egoism.[10] Unaided man's impotence to transcend self-regard and appetite is a commonplace of virtually every Christian tradition, whether orthodox or esoteric. Lewis and Barfield agreed that evil conduct brought about the soul's disintegration, but the former enjoined a passive "self-noughting" and active obedience to moral law, while the latter preferred "integrity" in his sense of actions characteristic of the individual. Like Steiner, he affirmed at this time that Man is his own law-giver.

PART THREE:
KEY ISSUES EXPLORED

CHAPTER 7

Imagination and Truth

Modern English resists abstractions. English lawyers more readily discuss "rights" than "Right" or "the Good." Wordsworth prefers "truths that wake to perish never" to "Truth Eternal." He thereby implies not a mind-made entity but truths that spring to life like undying creatures. In our age, we find it easier to understand "what John thinks" than "the thoughts of John" or, *a fortiori*, "ideas of John's mind." Likewise, "what John imagines" conveys more to the average modern English-speaker, especially if he be English, than "Imagination within John's soul." This ingrained empiricism of their language largely accounts for the difficulty English readers find in understanding the ideas even of German philosophers more academically respectable than Steiner.

In quite different ways this linguistic preference affects both contestants in the "Great War." Lewis cannot grasp the notion of "Truth" as an entity above and beyond "true statements." Barfield dislikes the convention of the syllogism by which some living and changing object is torn from its context and treated of as a still-life. For him, truth is something that comes to be.

The explosive charge of Lewis's opening salvo in the *Series I* letters is this distrust of abstractions. Equating Steiner's categories of "sensible" and "supersensible" with Plato's "phenomenal" and "real," Lewis, as will be recalled, finds supposed manifestations of the supersensible world delusory appearances and the "sensibilia" alone real. Even while rejecting Lewis's nominalism, Barfield for his part disagrees with Plato in that he finds the "sensible" world as real as the "supersensible." For this reason he, like Steiner, has always described himself as an Objective Idealist.

With perceptible relief—even, in comic sketches, with relish—Lewis turns from the absolute reality that reason cannot know to the practical substitute for knowledge that reason, experience and habit offer. In distinguishing between "object or fact" and "mental complex" thereto related, he restates a post-Kantian commonplace, the sundering of subject from object, "I" from "the world," but characteristically expresses it in grammatical as well as philosophical terms: "I say a complex," he begins in Letter II of *Series I,* "because when we know, we always know *that,* etc. (an accusative with the infinitive), i.e. we recognise a whole of parts, or a unity in diversity: of a mere one, I do not think there is knowledge unless you mean ... acquaintance." By implication, the accusative-infinitive construction applies only to statements in settled and known terms.

To illustrate Lewis's point, it is true that there is no fire without oxygen and false that phlogiston exists. Yet until we can imagine fire and attach some meaning to "oxygen" and "phlogiston" we cannot verify or falsify either assertion. But to speak of "fire" as that which "burning objects" have in common involves a capacity for perceiving and abstracting an element common to otherwise diverse appearances. Without the power to imagine, in the sense of "to form mental pictures," we could attach no meaning to "fire." The pictures our minds form need only amount to memory-images, for the act of re-creation within the mind implicit in Steiner's term "mental picture," or Coleridge's "secondary imagination," or Barfield's "representation," would be demanded only of the artist or creative writer.[1] In *Poetic Diction* Barfield alludes to the lack of a verb "to cut" in some primitive languages, as distinct from "cut skin" or a generic term "tree" as distinct from "oak" or "cedar." This and my example of fire would doubtless serve as instances of what Lewis, in *Summa* II, xv, calls "the great primary abstraction."

Now only by what Barfield (in *Series I*, Letter IV) calls an "arbitrary and unknowable symbolism" can "oxygen" denote a real substance and "phlogiston" a non-existent one. Even to call phlogiston "imaginary" would be a contradiction in terms, for our only ground for denying its existence is our inability to picture it or trace its effects. On the same ground, a linguistic analyst might deny meaning to the term "God" or a modernist theologian call for a new image of God. Even the analytical philosopher, however, might be cautious about committing himself to the statement "Belief in God is untrue."

Lewis refuses to attribute truth or falsehood to bodies, feelings, imagination or images, however lifelike. Since, as both disputants agree, images appear only as poetic "imagination" ebbs, Lewis can only allow that truth might conceivably pertain to some imageless condition "wherein the light of sense goes out." At any rate, he considers, the terms "true" and "false" cannot apply to utterances or beliefs remaining in the mind as imagination fades. Even if they could, whatever assertion resulted could differ from a normal judgment only in being made with due emotion. A state of imagination, Lewis maintains, can be linked with any consequent judgment only in an "infra-logical" way, by blind association, for "granting the truth of poetical imagination, we can never argue from it to the truth of any judgment which springs up in the mind as it returns to normal consciousness." Since "the crossing of the frontier" from imaginative to normal consciousness

74

could as easily be marked by confusion of the two modes "as when you change the focus of your telescope," it follows that any "sedimentary assertions" must be no more or less true than any other statements.

Indeed, continues Lewis, states of intense imaginative awareness can give rise to conflicting certainties: "I have returned from inspiration—but very possibly I have never known it at all—sometimes convinced of the insignificance of the human spirit in the scheme of things, and sometimes of its divinity as lord of space and time and creator of all it seems to be enslaved to." To say that an accurate recollection of the inspired moment would show us that these opinions were symbols of some "concrete truth that transcended them both" would be to concede the case. For if "truth of imagination" does so differ from "normal truth" then "imaginative vision cannot be invoked as a source of certainty." Lewis concludes that "what lends its support equally to opinions that are contradictory . . . can really lend no support to *either*." He illustrates his judgment by playing off quotations. If from reading Wordsworth's "huge and mighty forms that do not live like living men" he emerges feeling "How likely that such things are," he might on the same day read Bacon [*sic*] on human life as "like a froward child that must be played with and humoured to keep it quiet . . . till it falls asleep, and then the care is over" and think "all our spiritual activities but a keeping ourselves snug and warm for a few minutes in this steppe of matter"[2] (*Series I*, Letter II).

Lewis never knowingly violated his rationalist principle that assertions needed proof by reasoning from established facts, but an important question, that cannot be answered here, is whether in his own spiritual progression or in his apologetics he ever unwittingly used imaginative experience as a ground of conviction.

To deny the legitimacy of ascribing a truth supposedly attained through imagination to "any concept or image which has happened (perhaps quite fortuitously) to cling to the moment in which the inspiration occurred" is not to dismiss poetry as mere fantasy or falsehood. Yet Lewis refuses to call poetry veridical and makes much of Sidney's claim that poets never lie, since they never assert. Lewis suggests that aesthetic experience may have its own value, one independent of truth. In obvious allusion to the statement in *Poetic Diction* that an act of poetic creation amounts to a gain in knowledge, Lewis asks whether Barfield, prepossessed with Truth as sole absolute, would "affirm that if Beauty will not be taken on as a door-keeper to Truth . . . her occupation must be gone?" Inconsistently, however, Lewis at once endorses Kant's advocacy of moral good as the one supreme value, for "we feel obliged to abandon proffered truth as well as proffered beauty in favour of doing, as soon as an interrupting duty knocks at our door."[3] The real value of imagination, he suggests, may lie in its giving "an enriched and corrected will."

To epitomise the whole disagreement about imagination and truth, one might describe Lewis as by instinct a noun-user and Barfield as a verb-user. To Lewis, imagination is a state he is "in," "during" a time, "after" which he "emerges." As a lover of *The Prelude*, he could be taking as his model that passage in which, by "listening to notes" that are "the ghostly language of the ancient earth" Wordsworth gains "visionary power" after which

> the soul
> Remembering how she felt, but what she felt
> Remembering not, retains an obscure sense
> Of possible sublimity.[4]

As "those fleeting moods/ Of shadowy exultation" result, in Wordsworth's view, from the growth of "faculties" that "have something to pursue," so Lewis concludes that imagination is a state, indicating some underlying reality behind appearances ("something that appears"). That reality, however, only reason can define and verify. Moreover, Lewis conceives of knowledge as a thing rather than a process, as a body of facts and judgments.

Barfield has rejected these assumptions not only in this controversy but in well-nigh all his subsequent books. This rejection forms the core of his central and subversive affirmation. What he has tried to subvert is the sole dominion of the rational, "prosaic" principle that "can increase understanding and true opinion but can never increase knowledge."[5]

In Letter IV Barfield locates the "great divide" between the disputants in Lewis's separation of "fact or object" from related "mental complex." He continues: "Truth to you . . . is something you *look at* . . . while reality is something you *are* but never *see*." In his own view, as already noted, truth is not an "accurate copy or reflection" but "reality taking the form of human consciousness." In this view of philosophical truth—as distinct from everyday judgments—there is "no distinction possible between the thought and the object thought of."

Barfield illustrates his elusive statement in a diagram to which he supplies the following gloss:

For *Nous* read Spirit, the underlying reality. From this become *gignetae*, "things known," including the knower himself and what he perceives. Inspiriation, or "supersensible" experience, "light of sense going out," etc., is a sort of withdrawal from A into that-which-is-in-process-of-becoming-A, wherein I find that I am also in (i.e. become one with) that-which-is-in-process-of-becoming-B.

In other words, inspiration to Barfield is an inward withdrawal from our everyday selves to some primal level of reality (*to on*) that is the ground, origin or potency (*dynamis*) of both the self and those things it normally experiences as being "other" than itself.

In the margin, Lewis notes: "Can you ever *be* anywhere else! and if it's a question of *finding 'that'* you are, that is *Knowing* + Accus[ative] + Infin[itive]." By this, he means that one can only withdraw into one's own inner being.

If Barfield is right, both subject and object, what we enjoy and what we contemplate, are grounded in a primal reality that includes them both. Conversely, this primal reality surfaces in our consciousness and we can train ourselves to attend to it. Truth, in the common phrase, "comes to mind." Barfield has subsequently illustrated this underlying oneness of subject and object by pointing to the mineral and vegetable ingredients of the human body.[6]

In Letter IV Barfield maintains that a term in a syllogism presents itself as an "arbitrary cross-section of a process in time" and therefore "changes with the person who thinks it." (To supply an extreme example of his point, "Men cannot fly to the Moon" would have been a safe major premise not long ago.) To make a proposition meaningful, its terms must be "artificially taken out of time and deposited on an imaginary shore in the land of Nowhen, while the whole thundering torrent of reality . . . is quietly impounded in *ceteris paribus*." This objection to fixed terms underlies both his attack on logical positivism in the second preface to *Poetic Diction* and his thought-provoking chapter on "Outness" in *What Coleridge Thought*.

Foundations laid, Barfield turns to the role of imagination. Can "knowledge" and "truth," he enquires in Letter IV, be ascribed to explicit (*"hoti"*) formulations only, or to what we imagine also, or else, as he prefers to believe, to the inspiration-imagination complex alone. Inspiration he sees not as irrational but pre-rational, to rational formulation as flower to fruit. This has become a commonplace of Jungian psychology, but Barfield illustrates it by an unusual analogy. How did Dante's Sun, he asks, acquire our modern sense of "a sun," one fixed star among many? Clearly, he answers, "some individual having in his mind (i) a pictorial image of the Copernican solar system and (ii) a pictorial image of some fixed star with planets, etc., suddenly *fuses the images together* (Greek *eis hen plattei*) by means of that faculty which Coleridge accordingly dubbed 'esemplastic'." Introspection reveals this to be the origin of fresh meaning, that distinguishes truth from truism. The process that Barfield describes, along with the denial of induction as prime basis of scientific discovery, forms a pillar of Karl Popper's then little known theory of discovery by falsification.[7] According to Popper, hypotheses depend on no previous process of fact-collection, but may come about through some leap of imagination. If and so long as they survive attempts to show them inadequate to explain facts, they remain provisionally true. All truth, therefore, is provisional and progress in science results not from verification but from falsification. Popper's work, published in German in 1934, became well-known in English-speaking countries only after his departure from Austria in 1937. Needless to say, Barfield has never subscribed to Popper's scientific positivism but did in this one respect anticipate his findings.

Terms, Barfield continues, "perpetually tend to lose their meaning and become tautologous" but meaning is "renewable at the fount of inspiration, flowing through imagination to analogy, and thence either (a) into metaphor and so poetry, or (b) into hypothesis and so science." Not long afterwards, he added a passage to his thesis describing the "fashionable contrast between Poetry and Science" as destined to become "a source of wonder" to posterity and "of tragedy to ourselves," and criticizing the authors of that then new work *The Meaning of Meaning* as "rigid under the spell of those verbal ghosts of the physical sciences, which today make up practically the whole meaning-system of so many European minds."

Barfield even discerns for imagination a role in syllogism-construction, for it "blossoms" into the minor premise. "I may know already that all hippopotamuses have pink intestines, but only a free operation of 'esemplastic' imagination can enable me to assert triumphantly '*This* is a hippopotamus'." What he means, as he shows by citing Mill on resemblance as a ground of inference,[8] is that imagination always involves perceiving similitude, so that in a minor premise it operates to judge "in the sense of *actus judicandi* rather than *res judicata*." This intuitive act can only become a fixed "judgment" by being "stamped out" into a verbal statement applicable to whole classes of objects and therefore liable to error. This possibility alone constrains Barfield to agree with Lewis on the invalidity of arguing from "truth of poetical imagination" to "truth of any judgment which springs up in the mind as it returns to normal consciousness."

The scientist, Barfield implies, can verify hypotheses by experiment, but because the modern poet has no equivalent way to ascertain how far his achieved metaphors may correspond to reality, his "fantasy," a "screen of his accidental self" can distort the reality he observes.[9] The poet can overcome this tendency only by learning to retain his full power of discrimination "at the imagination or *actus judicandi* stage ... as at the *hoti*" or explicitly judgmental stage of thinking. Since his mind has never abandoned normal consciousness, he incurs no risk of error through return to full physical awareness. Barfield illustrates in a group of simple diagrams this mental discipline of "systematic imagination" known among anthroposophists as "occultism." He notes beneath an explanatory paragraph that Lewis has erred in alleging that occultism supplies further so-called phenomena, for Lewis has mistaken metaphoric descriptions for phenomena.

Barfield's conceptions of truth and meaning presuppose a primal, unitive reality, a One that fathers forth the many objects that to most of us constitute reality. In creating his myths, prehistoric man presumably expressed a "given" meaning implicit within his environment, one not subject to distortion through individual predilection. It follows that Barfield views knowledge not as a collection of established facts but as an act of knowing implicit in the dead metaphors "see," "grasp," "understand" and "conceive." To imagine is to make connections, to close circuits (Barfield is apt to use electrical metaphors).

This approach to knowledge, one more evident in Greek, Scholastic or Zen metaphysics than modern philosophy, seems applicable only to creative thinking. Yet every lecturer or pleader worth his salt knows from experience that he cannot profitably convey even factual information until he has applied himself to organising it into, as we say, a "body" of knowledge. To organise means literally to make alive, to endow with form and meaning. In Lewis's frame of reference, however, only the original deposit of fact could be deemed "true"; the organising activity or the images into which the imagination organised facts could at best be termed "meaningful." Any consequent assertions could, of course, be true or false. Barfield, as an Aristotelian, would consider any originating material truth potential (*dynamis*) but not truth actual (*energeia*) until the imagination had acted upon it in the way of knowing or understanding.

In Letter V Lewis, unconvinced, asks whether Barfield can still agree that neither images "connected with a moment of imagination" nor any concepts need not be and usually are not copies of "anything existing *in rerum natura*"; that the "moment of imagination" cannot therefore attest the truth of any assertion suggested by resultant images or concepts, and therefore it cannot be "cited as *evidence* for any *assertion*" not arising from the mere fact of its occurrence. Images, then, have reality simply as events in the individual mind.

Moreover, Lewis flatly refused to believe in Barfield's primal Reality (for short, "R") that was potentially (*dynamei*) one with a given object ("R2") beheld in actuality (*energeia*). His ground of disbelief can only be inferred from Barfield's reply to a missing letter. Barfield explains how becoming aware of a previously unrealised motive can fuse conscious and unconscious

79

wishes into one. He then reproves as "static" thinking Lewis's assertion that to know a being is not to know its embryo, so only the being that presently appears (R2) can be known as "real." To explain to Lewis how the mind can know both itself and an underlying Reality (R), Barfield asks him to imagine being informed that the glass through which he has always looked is coloured. After rubbing off the pigment, he would see reality more perfectly but the pigment he scraped off would remain part of reality, though of primary concern to Lewis himself. A moment's reflection will show us the fundamental importance of Barfield's analogy for Lewis's final awareness that the twentieth century is a period with its collective assumptions neither more nor less sacrosanct than those of other periods. This Lewis acknowledged as the most valuable lesson he learned from his "Great War" with Barfield.

Evidently Lewis added some elaborations of his own in letters now lost, for in Letter VII he complains of being misunderstood. "My scheme was *Hills*=the Real . . . , *Glass*=finite personality, categories, forms of sense, sensuous machinery. *Picture as seen in glass*= . . . 'the phenomena to the man X'." He had thought both disputants "believed in the *Ding-an-sich* in the sense that if there is appearance there is something that appears." Avowing that "I, at any rate, don't accept a world of pure smoked glass," Lewis offers his own version of the analogy. To attain knowledge of the Real is to wipe the smoke from the glass and thereby change the observer's view, not the object he observes. Unless "real" be understood as "the single and unchanged . . . source of varying phenomena" and "of each individual's private phenomena," Lewis sees no meaning in the term save "those parts of an essentially erratic, subjective experience which you happen to like."

Doubtless the outside observer sees what the disputants mean "through a glass darkly." Barfield seems to intend the glass to represent the senses through which all men perceive, the pigment to represent whatever private conditioning factors may affect the observer's vision (since someone who sees more plainly can advise him to remove it), and the observer himself to gain in wisdom from becoming aware of the pigment and from seeing the world uncoloured. To remove the pigment—which, after all, forms part of reality —is not to shed an illusion but to realise how personal experience and emotion have affected one's view of the world one now views objectively. As a developing organism, one remembers one's former subjective view. By the erasure, however, one has modified the environment and so become in part its creator as well as its perceiver.

By modifying the substance, which he calls "smoked" (not "coloured") glass, Lewis emphasises his belief that the change of consciousness amounts simply to the removal of an illusion in the individual observer, without modification of the "real" world outside. Neither he nor Barfield would agree with Hume, or many a Buddhist philosopher, that what the human senses disclose need not be real at all. Lewis sees the individual developing, rather in isolation, against an unchanging reality. Barfield views the individual as inevitably participating in a changing reality, though best able to perceive the part lying outside his own body.

Since Barfield's primal reality includes mind, he is a Jungian rather than a Freudian. He divides the process of knowing into four phases: Reality, Inspiration, Imagination and Judgment. He attributes truth to the process by which reality arises from a womb-like or oceanic state that precedes and generates both object—perceived phenomena (Greek for "appearances")—and the subject perceiving, so that the subject can ultimately state explicitly the nature of the phenomena. But first the subject must *imagine* the diverse phenomena ("the Many") by realising their essential oneness with each other and with himself. To do this, like Coleridge's water-insects swimming upstream,[10] he must perfect the discipline of returning to that wordless, imageless state in which he and they are one.

Lewis, on the other hand, views imagination as a power enabling us to make pictures more or less accurately corresponding with phenomena external to ourselves. Without thus giving the phenomena form and meaning, the mind could never arrive at true judgments. Residual mental pictures may or may not correspond with whatever the mind has previously imagined. Their existence cannot vouch for the truth of any conclusions the mind draws, which must be validated on the traditional grounds of logical coherence and correspondence to collectively observable phenomena. Imagination as Lewis envisages it amounts to the subject's "wise passiveness" before the object. This assurance of things "actually out there" was to him a psychological necessity.

While the disputants did not suddenly or dramatically move out of their entrenched positions, Barfield re-examined his assumption that the mind could observe its own thinking and eventually agreed—like Steiner, Wordsworth and probably Coleridge—that it could do so only in retrospect. He also became intensely preoccupied with the question "In what way is imagination true?"[11]

In *Surprised by Joy*, Lewis recalls that once he came across Alexander's distinction between the contemplated and the enjoyed it seemed "self-evident" that "the one essential property of love, hate, fear, hope or desire was attention to their object." To cease attending to a woman was to cease loving; to cease attending to a thing feared was to cease being afraid. "But to attend to your own love or fear is to cease attending to the loved or dreaded object." No doubt, he had in the meantime read a finely-expressed statement of a converse fact of the mind in the *Theologica Germanica*:

> The two eyes of the soul of man ... cannot both perform their work at once: but if the soul shall see with the right eye into eternity, then the left eye must close itself and refrain from working, and be as though it were dead. For if the left eye be fulfilling its office toward outward things; that is, holding converse with time and the creatures; then must the right eye be hindered in its working; that is, in its contemplation.[12]

He stood his ground also in maintaining that imagination and truth belonged in different categories. In his paper "Bluspels and Flalansferes" read several years after the "Great War," he defined imagination as "the organ of meaning ... which is the antecedent condition both of truth and falsehood, whose anithesis is not error but nonsense." Imagination, he concluded, "producing new metaphors, or revivifying old, is not the cause of truth, but its condition." By the time he wrote the fine passage on Imagination in the *Summa*, he must have accepted much of Barfield's belief concerning the importance of imagination and the underlying oneness of subject and object.[13]

CHAPTER 8

Tools of Imagination

Their many Oxford contemporaries who spent summer evenings on tennis-courts and cricket-fields might have thought Lewis and Barfield distinctly odd for disputing interminably about imagination. Barfield's interest they might have understood, for he did have one book out and another under preparation. No outsider could have understood how deeply the still-maturing Lewis needed to view his own life as a work of creative imagination. As his remarks on metaphor, symbol and myth will show, this need came from a far deeper source than the common human detachment he primly described as viewing "our actual sufferings as we now take the tragedies of the poets" (*Summa* II, xi).

While Lewis was composing the *Summa*, Barfield was complying with the request of his publishers to add a further chapter to *Poetic Diction* in order to broaden his discussion of "The Making of Meaning," which in Chapter VII he had confined to the poetic use down the ages of a single word, "ruin." A passage in the new chapter deals with the making of metaphor. Barfield has just said that provided we de not look back beyond the point at which "given" meanings first gave way to "created" meanings, "language does indeed appear historically as an endless process of metaphor transforming itself into meaning." Then he adds:

> Seeking for material in which to incarnate its last inspiration, imagination seizes on a suitable word or phrase, uses it as a metaphor, and so creates a meaning. The progress is from Meaning, through inspiration to imagination; inspiration grasping the hitherto unapprehended, and imagination relating it to the already known.[1]

By the end of the disputes over his thesis, if not before, Barfield meant by "Meaning" that which expresses the relations of objects to each other and to their knower. In primeval dreamlike consciousness, because experience was a timeless, seamless continuum, a word expressed simultaneously elements of meaning now conceived and expressed discretely. (To adapt Tennyson, who presumably understood the implications of *spiritus*, "the spirit" *also* meant "the breath.")[2] As maker (*poiētēs*), the poet intuitively senses forgotten relationships between objects and experiences that our increasingly analytic thought-processes have separated out. In his metaphor, by restoring these lost relationships, the poet freshens the meaning of whatver key-words he employs. In an era of "prosaic" consciousness—and the evolutionary drift is towards this—the poet fights against the tendency of words to bifurcate and wither into abstract and lifeless tokens of the living realities whence many of them arose. Words that retain this pristine expressiveness, this "given" meaning, Barfield terms "figurative." While breath and spirit still seemed one with the wind that blew without, *pneuma* connoted all three. Likewise, early man felt heart-sick or his bowels moved with compassion. A modern metaphor may flash upon the poet's mind with the seeming inevitability of primitive figuration, but since the poet has by conscious effort fashioned the context within which to employ it, his metaphor must be deemed "achieved."

Barfield opposed the tendency of modern intellectuals—especially behaviourists and other positivists—to regard the current meanings of the words they used as "given" and absolute. He regarded Lewis, then a rationalist, as among those who used words in this "static" way. He even accused Lewis of talking as though knowledge were "administered," like medicine, to a "purely passive recipient." Exasperated by the unsympathetically literal treatment his metaphors were receiving at Lewis's hands, Barfield exclaimed: "Man alive, you can't approach the mysteries of creation *except* by the use of poetic tact" (*Series I*, Letter VI). He parodied Lewis's literalism by imagining himself interrupting an oral reading of *Prometheus Unbound* to exclaim: "Stop! He says his soul is an enchanted boat. Right! Boat moves over water, therefore his soul must move over her singing. But that is absurd." He asks, "Would you have enough spirit to kick me downstairs?"

Whether or not he has represented fairly Lewis's concept of imparting knowledge, Barfield, in the same letter, defines his own: "the most a conversation can do—and above all a philosophic conversation—is for A, by uttering symbols which are the result of his inner activity, to bring it about that B develops a corresponding activity." By agreeing to argue about the nature of language, he maintains, the two have tacitly agreed to allow each other "that willing suspension of mathematical accuracy which constitutes philosophic faith."

Now since, as Barfield's striking illustration has shown, the images "sun" and "fixed star" belong together, the astronomer's imagination has discovered rather than invented their relationship. Barfield adds: "an activity of precisely this nature is at the back of every hypothesis, every addition to meaning." Since the same leap of intuition has provided the scientist with a hypothesis and the poet with a metaphor, each has by non-inferential means discerned a real relationship of parts within the universal whole.

In Letter VII, Lewis admits having under-estimated the extent and importance of metaphor, even in his own verse, but still considers metaphor "one of the most important tools of poetry" rather than its essence. To explain his own assessment, he compares "The Lord is my shepherd" with his own "prosaic" rendering "The Deity exercises a benevolent superintendence in human affairs." The latinate abstractions are to his mind "counters" standing for "an infinite number of concrete experiences." By comparison with the "real wealth" of actual experience, they amount to "credit, or paper money." These "skeleton-conceptions," however necessary at times, "live only in the light of the real which they represent." In returning to actual experience or "concrete imagination," we realise the meaning of these abstract terms, though only in part, "for the abridgement is usually general while the imagination is individual." Since poetry is "intensely semantic but not at all assertive," to imagine what a statement would mean no more vouches for its truth than for that of rival hypotheses under consideration by a scientist. Since, however, poetry brings out the "whatness" (in Aquinas' term the *quidditas*) of a given thought, it amounts to "something more than decorated prose."

In his biblical example, Lewis somewhat oddly discriminates between "Lord" as the only concrete term and "shepherd" as an abstraction which, however, supplies "the flavour of care and protection" and therefore the "whatness" lacking in "superintendence." Poet and reader, he says, have tacitly agreed to exclude the shepherd's commercial activities. After proposing alternative pastoral metaphors, Lewis defines the poet's task as "revivifying 'counters' . . . establishing a gold currency." Poetry, he concludes, must be "more accurate and concrete (less 'in the air') than prose."

After specifying other devices for ensuring concreteness, such as sensory detail, simile, analogy and rhythm, Lewis states as a general principle that to appreciate a metaphor the reader must be explicitly aware of the respect of comparison. To illustrate this principle, he invents a number of glosses for Shelley's "enchanted boat" metaphor. The boat's non-existence, its rarity, solidity, unlawful operation and liability to induce sea-sickness he regards as "hopeless" glosses; its precious cargo and danger in movement he finds "nearly so"; its speed and beauty strike him as "warmish" glosses and its ease of movement and capacity to impart a sense of effortless power as "pretty near."

Metaphor, Lewis warns, can prove ambiguous (to him, whatever Empson thought, a defect) if used as a means of argument. He has in mind Barfield's flower-and-pod metaphor. The function of a metaphor in argument, Lewis continues, "is subtle and delicate." A good enough metaphor might impart the "whatness" his opponent finds in knowledge without clearly defining that view or proving it well-founded. The question as to whether Barfield views knowledge rightly, Lewis adds, "is one of thatness: whether this 'what' which you present to me *is* actually given in instances which we should be prepared to call knowledge." A "whatness" can only be shared, by "sense or imagination," not agreed upon like a "thatness," for "whatness does not contain actuality: the bringing before the mind what X is, preliminary to the question whether X exists."

Notwithstanding Barfield's suggestion that philosophy originated in wonder, that is in potential knowledge,[3] Lewis insists that the best-chosen metaphor, proceeding from the best-exercised imagination, cannot of itself establish the truth of a statement. Hypotheses, whether "logistically contrived" or "flashed upon us by metaphor" can and do enable the enquirer to ask the right question, and in that sense "imagination is paramount" in enquiry. But to say that "imagination is knowledge" or that knowledge is of "whatness" seems to Lewis like saying that "to wonder is the same as to know, that there is no difference between doubting and discovering, that a question is the same as its answer, and that the solution of a problem is the problem itself." The poet, Lewis concedes, need not consciously think out the respect of comparison as if arriving at a judgment, for he may forge the metaphor by intuition and be conscious only that it "gives him the right feeling."

At that time I. A. Richards' valuable distinction between a metaphor's tenor and vehicle (content and illustrative image) had not become available, though Barfield has since used it to good effect.[4] Essentially, Lewis maintains that the link between tenor and vehicle must become explicit to the reader, if not the writer. To illustrate his point, and at the same time to suggest a reason why he attached far more importance to metaphor by the time he completed the *Summa*, I should like to consider a well-known passage in *Macbeth*.[5] When Macbeth pictures life as "a poor player/ That struts and frets his hour upon the stage," he clearly has in mind histrionic bombast and unreality, but the image "brief candle" has much wider connotations. That human life is transitory men have always known as a truism, but does Macbeth mean also that human life, like a candle in a dark room, subsists briefly in a meaningless and otherwise lifeless universe? *A priori*, we know only that Macbeth, bereaved and facing defeat, saw his own life as pointless. Only our total awareness of the play, that is of Macbeth within his context, can assure us even that this was his final conviction.

To know whether this was Shakespeare's view, we should need to find out whether any seventeenth-century dramatist was likely to have envisaged life in so sceptical and pessimistic a way. Even were this so, we cannot tell whether Shakespeare wrote subjectively as a temperamental pessimist, whether he echoed the disillusionment of an age or whether through Macbeth's soliloquy he conveyed an objective truth about life, for to a greater or less degree the enquirer's temperament and experience condition any answer. If for argument's sake we assume like Camus that life is "absurd," we shall see Shakespeare's candle metaphor as conveying a truth altogether more profound and more absolute than the mere truism "life is transitory," and conveying it whether or not Shakespeare believed or even realised what Macbeth was saying.

In that case, the general statement about life that forms the tenor of Shakespeare's metaphor—as distinct from the circumstance of Macbeth's bereavement—was a truth not then realised. Equally, however, a metaphor's tenor might be some truth, reality or circumstance in a buried individual or racial past. Neither the Freudian individual nor the Jungian collective unconscious seems to have been known to the two young scholars fighting the "Great War." Nor would either psycho-analytic concept account for a truth as yet unrealised, one not "buried" but "unborn," a truth potential (*dynamis*). Since our very example of unborn truth in the candle metaphor is suppositious, we can only safely infer *reality* forgotten or as yet unseen, something experienced or to be experienced rather than known or to be known.

In both his "Great War" letters and the chapter added to his thesis, Barfield points to a connection between metaphor and forgotten reality and, less specifically, infers one between metaphor and truth. How far he viewed metaphor as revealing "unborn" truth is not clear, as he does not, for example, discuss the now-familiar symbols in Blake's *Songs of Innocence* and *Songs of Experience*. To the challenge "What you imagine is not true," Barfield would conceivably have replied "It was, or will become so," but Lewis would certainly have replied "I never said it was. It arises from something I am or was experiencing."

Some such realisation, at all events, underlies the remarks in the *Summa* on myth, symbol and metaphor.[6] After defining the spiritual life as one enabling men to view their lives with the detachment of spectators watching a tragedy, Lewis distinguishes between two kinds of art. "Fiction, or Feigning" provides objects we can regard with detachment and completely understand. "Technē," the craft of expression, permits "transference ... of any experience in its concreteness" as distinct from the mere "statement" or "conceptual element" of the experience. Because "imaginative experience" transcends mere conception, "imagination is *par excellence* the content of Art" and Art "*par excellence* the vehicle of imagination." (Here Lewis comes very close to anticipating Richards' terminology.) Art and imagination, however, are not identical, for in Art, specifically the novel and "much of the Drama," the fictional element ("Feigning") outweighs the imaginative. (Lewis does not explain in what way fiction fails to be imaginative.) The craft of expression employs not only words and shapes, but also "fictions or stories" that produce "the same imaginative experience which may elsewhere occur in the presence of phenomena." To imaginative fiction consciously created by the artist Lewis gives the generic term "symbolism," and to that created "unconsciously by the people" he applies the term "myth." While any great work of art will probably include pure "Fiction," "Fiction as expression" and "pure expression," Lewis designates the novel and the drama as the "special domain" of Fiction, the epic and Mārchen as domains of "Fiction as expression, symbolically or mythically used," and, of course, lyric poetry and music as products of "pure expression."

Lewis could hardly for long have remained satisfied with his Crocean definition of lyric poetry. Of more permanent interest is his treatment of fiction. He seems to be distinguishing romance from naturalistic fiction. The former he regards as imaginative in that it presents a world created, or at least re-shaped, by the author; the latter he refuses to call imaginative because it presents a world reproduced from actuality. He does not consider just how naturalistic fiction differs from non-fiction or from the making of a reflection or accurate copy of what the author has in mind, which in the *Series I* letters he has implied to be the function of imagination. He applies the term "symbolism" not to the almost illimitably connotative images of Blake or Yeats, but to consciously devised "fictions." As a lover of Shelley and Maeterlinck, he presumably has in mind those works, ranging from *Alastor* and *Prometheus Unbound* to *The Bluebird*, in which the writer expresses his deep moral conviction in a consciously-woven fantasy or re-worked myth.[7] On the whole Lewis proves a better guide to myth than fiction, probably because he is more at ease in dealing with stories whose meaning resides in their personages and events rather than in the artist's formulation and personal background.[8]

In *Summa II, xx*, Lewis relates myth and symbol to metaphor. In all three cases, "an experience of one kind" is "expressed, and enriched, by the supposal or suggestion (not the actualisation) of an experience of another kind." Because the author who imaginatively experiences a landscape "consciously co-operates with Spirit in making that landscape" he naturally writes in metaphors, for "Spirit experiences all things ordered and articulated in a perfect unity." Lewis postulates an "absolute relevance" perceived by Spirit, which "sees no object in isolation." In so far as we share Spirit's vision, we place each object we behold in its proper context; the "suggestion of that context," or rather what such "fragments" as "Space and Time" allow us to receive, "is metaphor."

From metaphor, Lewis argues, begins the "breakdown of isolation," but those fragments of "contextual experience" that become metaphors "need no experiences of the objective world." The reader of Keats' *Hyperion* can "see oaks more spiritually by seeing them as green-robed senators" even if Rome and its senators were "subjective fantasies" shared by poet and audience, for Spirit sees in unity not only the world but the fantasies of its inhabitants. As metaphors, such fantasies may enable us to "see the object more spiritually, that is, more really: but though they lend reality they do not receive it."

Despite the haziness of Lewis's terms "spiritually" and "really," his general drift is clear enough. Every object has some relationship to every other, and every metaphor exposes a patch of connective tissue. As maker of metaphors, the poet creates meaning by uncovering these relationships. By now, evidently, Lewis agrees with Barfield that a metaphor is, as Bacon says, among the "footsteps of Nature."[9] What Lewis and Barfield do not establish is a criterion for judging a metaphor's effectiveness, since in principle the poet is as free to expose a relationship between the moon and a piece of green cheese as between the moon and the tide. The one relationship certainly takes more discovering than the other, so that the poet's metaphor would be fresher, but appears no whit more real or more spiritual.

Lewis turns next to the effect of forgetting the origin of a group of metaphors. In this case, since their assemblage "was a taste of the unity of Spirit," he would still "enjoy imaginative experience" but would now apprehend the metaphors under the guise of "symbol or myth." This statement comes very near to identifying the "forgotten" and "unborn" truth in Macbeth's candle metaphor, but Lewis still reserves the term "truth" for what is objectively demonstrable, rather than subjectively experienced. As he insists, the fact that metaphor renders imaginative experiences more real does not prove them more than fantasies. Rather quaintly, he adds: "The existence of beings used as symbols (e.g. fairies, etc.) is therefore to be handed over to the sciences for empirical enquiry." Here he probably alludes to Steiner's willingness to accord as much credence to mythical as to historical beings, but might also be glancing at Yeats' folk-mysticism and theosophy.

What Lewis calls "myth" apparently subsists within particular souls, which enjoy "imaginative vision of they-know-not-what," for Spirit alone views all things in mutual relationship. He conjectures that they may "contemplate the metaphors enriching a certain experience, which . . . is for some reason withheld," and to this limited degree they may enjoy "the point of view of Spirit."

One might infer that since the Spirit that sees all things in context must see them truly, the soul that, within its limitations, discerns spiritually cannot but discern truth.[10] Nevertheless, moral considerations inhibit Lewis from allowing truth to either the imaginative experience or its fruits. Proof that mythic beings existed would destroy their symbolic value, for "the symbol is never *given* as a fact, but *taken* by free spiritual activity." If mythic beings actually existed, they would have "empirical" value as objects of fear, desire or other passions. Of this empirical value they would need to be stripped, or "disenchanted" before being "re-enchanted" by being regarded in a more "spiritual," that is more detached way. For this reason Lewis esteems fantasy rather than fact as a source for metaphor, and goes so far as to say that if all mythology were proven true, "the poets would throw it away and invent a new one, warranted untrue."

In his tortuous argument, Lewis restricts the meaning of "symbol" to what is invented or at least non-factual, "taken" rather than "given." This undercuts Barfield's main argument, in *Poetic Diction*, that the primal languages used in the earliest mythologies were more poetic than modern languages just because their words directly expressed the realities men experienced. What Lewis calls "free spiritual activity" Barfield would attribute to the modern poet's conscious employment of imagery in order to refresh the awareness of experience, both by himself and by his readers. Lewis, like Aristotle, thinks of the poet as maker rather than prophet or oracle.

He cites from Santayana (and possibly Macdonald) the idea that an object must be "disenchanted" of its emotional appeal before it can have spiritual or moral value.[11] To attribute absolute value to the content of a myth, he maintains, is "idolatry."[12] He is trying to subvert Steiner's veneration for mythology as a channel of revelation in order to preserve it as a source of pleasure and the emotional excitement he later calls "Joy" or "*Sehnsucht*."

After his conversion, Lewis changed his mind about myth, symbol and the moral value of fact. He composed an address on the Incarnation as "Myth that became Fact"[13] and insisted that even Christ's ethical teaching mattered less than the myth-like yet historical events of Christ's life, death and resurrection. Yet the Gospels never appealed to him, stylistically at least, and he grounded his theology in the Pauline and Augustinian scheme of salvation rather than the Jesus of the synoptic Gospels.[14] His motive may well have been personal, for having lost his mother in early childhood, he grew up in his father's sombre house, living most intensely when reading poetry or fiction, or playing out fantasies with his brother.[15] His mother, source and mainspring of his early happiness, had become a myth (as described in the

Summa), the forgotten object of his longing and misgiving, his *Sehnsucht*. In another sense she had become a symbol, that subterranean spring whence flowed the river of his imagination. By "forgotten" I mean not that he did not remember her but that he never, in youth at least, uncovered the thread running from his mother to his present feeling of "joy" not of this earth.

The external world Lewis viewed with disenchanted eye until 1929-31, his years of decision, during which he nursed his dying father, settled in his own house and found his spiritual home in traditional Christianity. In myth and romance he came to discern the operation of Spirit, "what I really am," and like Barfield vowed the spiritual life as a "coming-home."[16] Imagination was his organ of spiritual discernment, its tendons metaphor, myth and symbolism. He abandoned the *Summa*'s extreme anti-naturalism once, having laid his father to rest, he shed his guilt at his inner dearth of filial affection. Reconciled both to his earthly father's memory and to his heavenly Father (on whom he had more to say than on the Son and the Spirit), he could find enchantment in the woods and wild creatures near his home. Yet he could only present the Gospel drama in mythic guise in his Narnia fantasies, for he needed to translate it into the language of romance and declare it in the voice of symbol.

In discussing metaphor, the disputing friends are at cross-purposes, for Barfield retraces mankind's steps by listening to the footfalls that echo in language, while Lewis will recognise no sound but presently explicit speech. Yet Lewis has an unrecognised compulsion to trace his own path. To see all things in unity, as Spirit sees them, he must gaze at once upon the living and the dead. Like Macdonald's child-hero, Diamond, Lewis must peer behind the north wind.[17] Like Dr Johnson, another of his literary exemplars, he needs to be assured, however, that things actually are as he imagines and perceives, that real stones can be kicked through real windows. Faith in reason and external reality was, if anything, more essential for his peace of mind than faith in the unseen and transcendent.

CHAPTER 9

Self-Consciousness

Existential anxiety torments in many ways. In a Hopkins sonnet the damned know only their "sweating selves" and George Borrow's Lavengro doubts his own existence. Nowadays many a male student desires to "find himself" and many a female one to "preserve her identity." Neither self-loathing nor self-doubt troubled Lewis: rather, his anxiety was that of a prisoner in a darkened room of unknown shape and size, who needs to know whether there is solid ground beneath or wall behind him. Typically, one of his sketches depicts an anthroposophist in "*Chimaerarum terram*." Long after the "Great War" he remained troubled by the dissolution of solid matter and by the uncertainty principle in modern physics.[1] Barfield, by contrast, found comfort in theories supporting his belief that the subject, "I," is at one with the object, "the world," inasmuch as both consist not of solid matter but of opposed energies.[2]

Lewis, then, needed the reassurance of knowing perceiving subject and perceived object as distincts, while Barfield felt reassured by knowing them as one. Put as a proposition, Lewis's conviction "There is a world outside myself" contains five elements: (1) myself, (2) "is" (exists), (3) "a world" (phenomena), (4) some relationship between "myself" and "the world" and (5) some linking medium. In the *Summa* Lewis eloquently presents imagination as the medium, while in a number of books Barfield has argued the case for language, since it transmits not only the subject's awareness but the reality the subject perceives. Barfield's hall-mark as a philosopher has been his use of grammar and semantics to support his metaphysic, Objective Idealism,[3] in a period when philosophers usually employ linguistic analysis to discredit metaphysics. Lewis, though splendidly endowed, made no original contribution to philosophy, perhaps for the very reason that existential anxiety inhibited his mind from brooding upon its own nature and dissolving the solid surfaces of things, indeed from that kind of exploration existentialist theologians engage in. However lucidly argued, Lewis's case for traditional Christianity appeals primarily to enquirers who share his pre-romantic sense of the self's distinctness from its environment.

The first four elements in our imaginary proposition constitute the subject-matter of *De Toto et Parte*. Barfield's discussion of the self undoubtedly influenced Lewis, even perhaps to the extent of becoming a secondary source for the distinction made in *Surprised by Joy* between the contemplated, the enjoyed and the unconscious. As a Coleridgean, Barfield naturally wondered whether "contemplated" and "enjoyed" were mere synonyms for "object" and "subject." When in *Summa* II, viii Lewis compared Spirit to an artist and found Art less than fully spiritual because its objects might prove but "subjective fantasies," was he obliterating the line between subjective and objective? Had he but found new words for old concepts? Lewis replied that the subjective was "a special area of the contemplated." Besides contemplating external objects, each soul contemplated its private *"contemplata,"* for example mental images, which were indeed "subjective." Again, an "intermediary" (in Lewis's sense an author) who creates "souls-in-a-world" within himself may contemplate certain phenomena from the subjective viewpoint of those "souls." From the intermediary's viewpoint whatever they behold is subjective, for his objective world is the one he shares with his fellow-authors. From the viewpoint of any higher beings, the intermediary's world would itself be subjective. In a sketch, too allusive and complex for reproduction, Lewis depicts a series of links from Spirit, through higher intermediaries, to Barfield and thence to characters in Barfield's own fiction, whom he relates to Barfield as Barfield to supposed angelic intermediaries. The subjective-objective distinction, Lewis concludes, "has an important meaning, provided you explain 'For whom?' " (*Replies to Objections*, II, viii).

Barfield bases his explanation of our first term, "myself," on the axiom that consciousness can only be conceived as self-consciousness. He is aware of being one self, "subject of many experiences." Several of these experiences— sleep, terror and temptation—may suspend the sense of selfhood, yet in general he feels empowered to decide "whether Barfield shall be one or many." Since the integrated person has this self-consciousness, and since he "cannot integrate nothing," any increase in his self-consciousness involves an increase in the number and variety of his experiences. Barfield now distinguishes between stages in self-awareness. In his first "naive" stage, "the sum of my experiences took the form for me of a cosmos, or whole consisting of parts, of which parts myself was conceived to be one." In a further stage, he realised that he, "while remaining one of the parts," must be also *"in some sense,* the whole." This realisation, Barfield concludes, "enormously increased my conception of the extent to which integration is possible."

Because the growth of self-awareness has become such a predominant theme in the literature of the past two centuries, Barfield's remarks can easily be illustrated from fiction. In the opening chapter of *Great Expectations*, Pip's naming of objects within his purview leads to awareness of himself in a state of overpowering emotion. Then by stages Pip's dawning self-awareness is suspended in terror—in Freudian parlance "trauma"—during his encounter with the convict, until the self-recollecting adult narrator baldly records his child-self's words and actions. Ultimately the hero becomes in Barfield's sense a fully-integrated character, capable of assessing his own previous conduct as a preliminary to acting on his own responsibility, and feeling remorseful affection for the convict and his other benefactors. In attempting to mould Pip into "my gentleman," the convict has meantime acted out what Lewis would call a "subjective fantasy."

Again, Maggie Tulliver's sense of selfhood is momentarily suspended at the climax of her temptation to elope with Stephen Guest. So far as Maggie attains integration, she does so through "natural piety," her desire for an organic continuity between her beginning and her ending, as though her life were a work of art.

In this, Barfield's second stage, the earlier "naive" phase need not be renounced, for self-realisation depends on "interplay between . . . being the Whole and being a part (together with other parts)." Barfield has in mind neither egoistic detachment nor anonymous belonging, neither pebble nor clod, but what he has since called "conscious participation" in life. Merely being the whole (*pace* Lewis) cannot suffice, for awareness of self and not-self are complementary. Even in contemplating himself, he adds, he contemplates a self expressly "objectified." The "real and contemplating self" becomes conscious in the very act of contemplation. Were there no contemplated object, there could be no contemplation.

The difficult passage in *De Toto* #4 presents a logical problem. If self-consciousness implies awareness of not-self, then the self being "objectified" must be fictional, or at any rate other than the self that presently contemplates. If fictional, it could take the form of a spurious self-image, such as the "gentleman" archetype on which the "real" and mature narrator Pip continually implies judgment. More probably Barfield has in mind Steiner's *Vorstellung*, or still-life representation of an object in motion, the only means by which a living, changing person can view himself. Thus, as Coleridge says, the subject becomes his own object.[4] Our second interpretation makes sense only if the contemplating and contemplated selves exist in different planes, as with conscious and unconscious minds. But whereas a psycho-analyst brings his patient to contemplate a hitherto buried unconscious self, Barfield suggests that the contemplating self comes into existence in the very act of observing a self "objectified" as a still-life image. This contemplating self is the Ego that, in Steiner's teaching, has within the past few centuries emerged as the crowning achievement of human psychological evolution.

Barfield's definition of virtue as "integrity" in this sense of emergent self-awareness evidently conflicts with Lewis's ethic of self-renunciation, but the principle itself presents some difficulties. Barfield obscurely remarks that self-consciousness "is always awareness, *as* one, *of* many, or ... *being* one in and through many" and that "the more objects in which the subject realises itself as one, the higher is the degree of integration" (*De Toto* #4). It is not easy to pin down his meaning for "objects." A footballer cannot function in his own role without knowing the roles of his team-mates. The more complete his knowledge, the more he thinks and reacts *as* the whole team, and any team whose members entirely lack this corporate consciousness will suffer defeat and disintegration. For a similar reason, generals briefed their troops more fully in the Second World War than in the First. But does Barfield mean that a fully-integrated person cultivates awareness of his body's involuntary functions, or that such a person uses "objects" encountered in his own work and play, or that he uses other people as means of self-realisation? The Platonic terms "one" and "many" suggest a central organising consciousness that manifests itself in numerous roles, functions or aspects, but need these all be contained within the self? To what extent can one realise oneself in and through others?

Barfield resolves these difficulties in discussing our second element, "to be." In *De Toto* #5 he first defines the copula as "The thing is what it is, and knows nothing about it." He gives as examples "the horse is a quadruped," "the dream which my dog had last Monday," and "the centaur which I thought I saw last Tuesday." Truth and falsehood only apply once the question arises "Is what?" Barfield adds that "every division of the Many 'is' and ... this bare fact of being (... common to them all) ... I call 'the One'." Otherwise, he concludes, no whole can subsist without forming part of some larger entity. The copula in this sense appears synonymous with what Lewis calls "the Unconscious."

Barfield's second definition of being is a "necessarily conscious" state, such as love, pain or belief, in which "to be anything is in the same moment to know that I am it." In this sense, Barfield says, "I 'am' clearly only a part of the Whole that I can think about." In self-mocking vein, he adds that this will be his normal meaning throughout *De Toto* "and in all my subsequent philosophical writings."

The third sense of the copula represents a compromise between the first two: "one is something in the first sense and also believes or opines that one is it—*but not in the same moment*." One might, for example, have verified the previously unapprehended fact of descent from a given ancestor. From this Barfield concludes that "the principle of uniformity in Nature,"

"Reason" and "the law of identity" assure him that "I, inasmuch as I can truthfully say 'I think', 'am' the Whole that I can think about."

The first sense of "to be" therefore implies a state, the second a state *ipso facto* known and the third a state believed in. Barfield concludes in Platonic vein that to pass from mere being or from opinion to knowledge is to "realise" whatever one is.

This account of self-realisation answers our difficulty as to the "objects" by which the subject may realise himself as one. If the Many merely are, the One knows itself to be and the subject attains knowledge of his own being, then the objects by which he has attained this realisation must include formerly involuntary acts, past or present states reflected on, sensations, recollections, images and facts all known through being brought to mind. Barfield is thus equating integration with a necessary tension between, in Coleridgean terms, "multeity" of consciousness and a pervading unity.[5] We may infer that multeity alone would manifest itself existentially in schizophrenia, imaginatively in delirium and conatively in irresolution. Unity alone would respectively manifest itself in obsession, melancholic sterility and automatic response to stimuli. In a recent essay Barfield has discussed multeity in the light of R. D. Laing's controversial account of schizophrenia. As a neo-romantic critic he clearly has had in mind Blake's "single vision and Newton's sleep."[6] His whole concept of self-realisation accords with the "affirmative" tradition of mysticism, and leaves no room for "self-noughting" by rejection of images or activities. Lewis's "upward relapse into Spirit" and ethic of self-forgetfulness in duty accords better with the "negative way."[7]

Barfield always qualifies his observations on our third element—phenomena, matter, the cosmos—by saying "the Whole that I can think about." Lest he appear to limit discussion to that portion of reality within his purview, thereby implying some larger reality beyond, he stipulates, in the first of the definitions that end *De Toto*, that "there can be nothing beyond —no larger Whole inclusive of—" this "Whole that I can think about." He justifies this position by the argument that to suppose a further world is itself an act of "thinking about," so that the supposed world, even if non-existent, "is included in my cosmos."

Since "Spirit" and "good" connote "integration" and consciousness of and as the cosmic Whole, the state of mystical perception, Barfield considers, represents heightened rather than diminished self-awareness. In such moments one is laid asleep in body to become a living soul. Yet if aware of the Whole, one also knows oneself as subject and the surrounding cosmos as object. Spiritual awareness, being a part yet also the of Whole, is therefore more than normally "a union of thinking and feeling" (*De Toto* #7), for thinking (contemplation) pertains to the Whole and feeling (enjoyment) to the part. This dual awareness is, of course, more complex than Lewis's "seeing as Spirit sees," that is as the Whole only.

Within the cosmic Whole, Barfield notes, subject and object each include subsidiary wholes. If "the Whole that I can think about," he continues in *De Toto* #7, besides containing such "formal wholes" be one itself, then Spirit can best be defined as "the realisation of form." Barfield's next sentence is crucial: "For since I am part of a whole, which is all its parts, to realise that Whole as Form would also be to realise *my own* form." This awareness of Form, of a relation between whole and part independent of space and time, which "are always threatening to disintegrate me," constitutes self-realisation. The "intuition of form" or "imaginative experience" resembles *"being the whole."* In this state the soul may, in Lamb's words, "resolve itself into the element which it contemplates," or an author feel that some greater power wields his pen. Nevertheless, this state also resembles "being a part," for it enhances rather than diminishes consciousness. Apparently Barfield personally experienced this dual awareness, for he adds:

> In imaginative experience I am immediately aware, alike of *myself*, a being separate from the object, and of a being or Whole, which includes both that self and the object. Moreover ... to all who have any dealings with art ... the intuition of form resembles an unusually complete union of thinking and feeling. (*De Toto* #7)

Although Steiner taught that the imaginative thinker can project himself into the object, Barfield writes here not merely out of his awareness of anthroposophical teaching and romantic sensibility but from a depth of personal experience that gives authority to his ensuing remarks. The "intuition of form," he continues, "differs from its realisation" in being "partial, and therefore often apparently ... clouded and confused." Full realisation of form would reveal "*every* respect in which the whole is the part." Between this full awareness and its antithesis, unconsciousness, lie "all degrees and combinations," of which he specifies three. The mystic intuits "very extensive wholes in very restricted parts"; the "Aesthete" intuits "only small and relatively insignificant wholes"; and the "imaginative man" as mean between the other two somehow practises both modes. For his first definition Barfield obviously has in mind Blake's "eternity in a grain of sand," but his second, a generation before M. H. Abrams' *The Mirror and the Lamp*, suggests the present-day (or ancient Chinese) vogue for treating poems as self-explanatory artefacts, designated by Abrams as "objective" criticism.

97

Since "intuition of form" involves both thinking and feeling, Barfield discusses these antinomies in the "*Theoria*" that concludes *De Toto et Parte*. Without "thinking" (used as an abstract noun, after the German mode), he cannot conceive wholeness of any kind, cosmic or lesser. He adds without explanation that though the Whole includes every lesser whole, "the *term* Whole is on the contrary included *in* whole." Presumably this means that though we form part of the cosmos, our names for it form part of us. Since the Whole merely "is," adds Barfield, it means little to say "I am" the Whole: rather he would claim to "bear witness" to It, for "like light, It is everywhere and dwells in me . . . only so far as I dwell in It." The individual, he explains, never perceives his own thinking until it has become fused with his feelings and sensations. If anyone could abstract thinking from its psychic context, it would become "for souls, unconsciousness," but this can only be inferred as an unrealisable extreme, like a line that has length without breadth. What Barfield implies is that ideally thought is impersonal: anyone who could simply think, without also feeling and sensing, would lose consciousness of himself. Several people who thought simultaneously in this trans-personal way would think identical thoughts. Barfield therefore defines thinking as "whole being," a phrase he compares to the German verb *sein*. (By employing a verb rather than a noun, he implicitly defines "whole" as a noun and "being" as a participle.) Because he had devised his whole system of mental training to enable the anthroposophical initiate to attain this pure, abstract and detached reasoning, Steiner named his system Objective Idealism.

Feeling, Barfield continues, resembles thinking inasmuch as we can only feel *about* something, but it differs in that we are at once aware that we feel. The unattainable extreme of feeling would be mere sensation without duration or reference to any object, a mere *consciousness* as distinct from self-awareness or unconsciousness. Feeling therefore pertains to the part: to the extent that the part knows of any larger whole, it necessarily knows itself.

Barfield completes his definition of Feeling by grappling with the relation of subject and object. He divides existence, in the sense of being and simultaneously knowing, into three categories. His first, a part that exists for itself in that it has feeling and awareness, he terms the "subject." His second, a part existing for another part inasmuch as it is felt or observed, he designates as the "object." His third category he can but postulate. This is a percept or sensation minus the element of thinking implicit in the other categories. This "absolute limit of partness" he equates with "mere consciousness," just as he equates the extreme of Wholeness with unconsciousness. To this kind of existence neither the term "subject" nor the term "object" could apply. A part incapable of self-awareness, a stone for example, might form an element in the consciousness of another part and thus become to it an "object." Barfield's first category clearly corresponds to Lewis's term "the Enjoyed," his second to Lewis's "the Contemplated," but his third must be the antithesis of Lewis's "the Unconscious."

Barfield now suggests that to view subject and object as two related parts is to over-simplify. Spiritual life depends for its fulness upon two necessary tensions: between being a part and being a whole; and between feeling, the mode of existence of the part, and thinking, the mode of the universal Whole. To maintain "integrity," awareness of a coherent inner self, demands an effort of will.

In his long definition of Will (capitalized for treatment as an abstract entity),[8] Barfield calls it "that which sunders part from whole and from other parts." No effort is needed to be the Whole, since everything belongs to It. In that capacity, a thing *is*, and hence has *being*, but as it acts or suffers it becomes a part, needing a correlative part as patient or agent. Thus action is inseparable from "partness" and since action takes place through the exercise of Will, the Will sunders parts from each other and from the Whole.

The next stage of Barfield's argument illustrates the anthroposophical habit of hypostatizing mental states and treating them as living creatures. Because he has not created his own self-consciousness, some other will must have done so, one "from which I am not yet wholly sundered, or (in terms of the *Summa*) which I 'enjoy'." To identify this Will with the Whole, Barfield says, is "anthropomorphism," for by "the Whole" he means "that which is." It follows that "apart from Dionysius and Aquinas and Steiner and tradition generally," there must be "a will or wills intermediate between myself and the Whole." Barfield argues further that since increasing self-consciousness brings increasing realisation that self-consciouness must be maintained by a personal act of will, "this unknown alien will is in process, if I choose, of becoming *my* will."

From this deduction, any student of Lewisian apologetics can understand why Lewis called Barfield his "unofficial teacher." Barfield, however, seems to discuss self-consciousness as an entity someone has created. By postulating intermediate "wills," he seems to enjoy at once the blessings of pantheism and belief in a personal deity, of determinism and freewill.

As the intermediary relates to the subject, so the subject relates to other parts, whose separateness from the Whole depends not on their will but on his. This act of separating out objects results from logical analysis, "from which, in my experience as soul, my self-consciousness finally sprang." The apparent contradiction between this statement and Barfield's earlier remark "I am not aware of having created my self-consciousness" is resolved by his account, in *Poetic Diction* and elsewhere, of how logical analysis and the separation of the psyche from its environment form a necessary stage in human evolution.

In summary, because the Whole merely "is," Will necessarily pertains to a part and is thus "dysemplastic," producing "not One from Many, but Many from One." Evidently Barfield has in mind the Coleridgean concept of the separative projection" of living organisms from a common ancestor or source, a process he has most notably traced in his philological writings. In this context, however, he is discussing ethics, especially whether a definition of virtue as "integrity," or self-consistency, implies egoism. He answers this question rather obliquely, by suggesting that while "my only duty is to be myself," the state of virtue is a conscious realisation—rather than a mere assumption—that all parts constitute One Whole. Hence the religious man, who values Being above mere action, "rightly gives to God the glory of all his virtue," indeed "knows that true virtue, inasmuch as it is simply *being* itself, is the free gift and condescension of heaven." He must will yet cannot earn this state, but "provided that there is a being to descend to, God will descend to that being from heaven." Barfield once more invokes the principle of polarity common to many post-Enlightenment metaphysicians. Virtue, he concludes, resides between two complementary antitheses, being a part and, by divine grace, discovering one's participation in the cosmic Whole. "Ethically, such a discovery . . . is *grace*; cognitively it is *revelation*. All genuine art is revelation and all genuine religion the result of it."

In repeating this Coleridgean assertion of a necessary tension between opposites, Barfield shows himself in one sense more modern than Lewis, in another sense less so. If virtue as integrity be an existentialist conception, art as revelation smacks of those ancient and medieval authors who, as Barfield has pointed out, believed their ideas to have been inspired (breathed into them) from above. Lewis, though ethically and theologically more conservative, always viewed artistic creation in a post-romantic way as the product of "imagination," that is, of the individual psyche. Barfield has striven to restore the older meaning of inspiration, but has also tried to build a bridge between older and newer views of creativity by postulating an "evolution of consciousness" through which modern man has become personally responsible for his ideas and images, whereas his ancestor had them "breathed into" him from the natural and spiritual environment.[9]

CHAPTER 10

Form, Will and Meaning

In order to determine how Barfield and Lewis view the relation of subject and object, we have been examining their use of the terms "myself," "is" and "the world." It remains for us to consider how Barfield, in particular, accounts for the mutual relationship between these elements, and for the growth of language, by which that relationship is expressed.

According to Barfield, the two essentials for this relationship of subject and object are Will and Form. Whereas in the *Summa* Lewis condemns the subject's will to subsist independently of Spirit, in *De Toto* Barfield finds will essential to the subject's individual existence. He stipulates, however, that the subject must both will his separateness and participate in the cosmic life. These two apparently contradictory but actually complementary acts he calls Will and Form, employing abstract nouns in a fashion more German than English.

Barfield's notion of Form emerges from his discussion in *De Toto* of whole and part, the One and the Many. He refers to no mere aggregation, as of X-million grains in a sand-heap, but to an organic relationship by which "each part, taken separately, expresses or contains the whole." As a bone-splinter or fir-cone reflects the structure of the entire animal or tree, so each part of a great poem or symphony proclaims the whole imagined by the artist before or during composition.

Time and space, being constituents of aggregative wholes, play no part in the intuitive appreciation of the organic relationship of a whole with its parts, that is, of formal structure. In a material or temporal sense "the wholeness of the Ninth Symphony and the Last Supper differs in no respect from that of a heap of sand or so many ticks of a clock." The artist's skill depends on his overcoming the wholeness of "mere aggregation and succession" with the "other wholeness" characteristic of art. Barfield cites Schiller on "the secret of the master's art, that the matter is annihilated through the form."[1] We progress in aesthetic appreciation, Barfield adds, in so far as we regard works of art less as matter and more as form. We become more imaginative as we regard not only artistic but natural objects in this way.

As previously noted, Barfield regards the individual as both a part of and a subsidiary whole within the cosmic Whole. Individual wholeness, "integrity," resides in a self-consciousness preserved by will-power from erosion by time and space. Since will thus "sunders" part from Whole and other parts, how can self-consciousness, the "sundering" itself, "make possible the realisation of Form?"

Will and Form, Barfield argues, are polar opposites, the "undemonstrable foundations on which all demonstration ultimately rests." He adds mysteriously that will therefore underlies not only self-consciousness but "the whole edifice of science, which it holds together at every joint," or rather "holds the edifice *apart* and prevents it . . . from crumbling together into mere being— mere unrealised Form."

Barfield intended explaining this in projected "Notes on the Definitions of Form and Soul," but since he never completed *De Toto* we can only infer his meaning from his definition of Form. Here he repeats that his definition, "the whole being a part," cannot be demonstrated but only expounded, and refers Lewis to a "Note on Intuition" apparently never written.

What Barfield does say is that although we experience by our feelings and sensations the existence of "an infinite multiplicity" of separate parts, we can by reasoning convince ourselves that through the "principle of identity," the uniformity distinguishing Nature from chaos, "one-ness of the One is everywhere at every moment." This kind of assertion he regards as not subject to empirical verification but inferrable from immediate experience. As a Neoplatonist, he regards self and not-self as mutually necessary polar opposites. By contrast, the majority of Existentialists would go beyond Keats' famous statement that one forms an "identity" by learning to cope with a "world of circumstance" not immediately comprehensible. They would find the subject and object intrinsically unrelated, the cosmos without any form that concerns us.

Barfield jettisons the Platonic nomenclature, the One as "reality" and the Many as "appearances." The intellect's very nature and function, he declares, is to assert the identity of the Many with the One. The truism "whatever is, is" implies that "the One is everywhere at every moment . . . the Whole is each of its parts." Here he has in mind *to on* (literally "the being") the Greek term for reality. This identity of Whole with parts, he says, can be grasped only by an aspect of the psyche "sufficiently sundered from that other part called logic or discourse to . . . contemplate this latter part not only as process but also as form—i.e. as the image of self-consciousness in soul."

If, however, the Whole merely "is" and "is" each of its parts in a bare copulative sense, must not this definition of Form stultify all logic, including Barfield's? His striking reply to his own objection is that "Form is illogical because it is on the ground of all logic." As Aristotle remarked, the ground is groundless or self-grounded. Logic, Barfield claims, is "a process by which all the parts are predicated of other parts and ultimately of the Whole. The validity of this process depends on the fact that "the Whole in its turn is those parts." We might from celestial motions infer a law of gravity, but neither from those motions nor from that law can we infer "the self-poised equilibrium" of the whole universe. To expect the universe itself to obey the gravitational pull of something beyond is nonsense, for "the universe as a self-sustaining whole is simply a fact. So is the form of the cosmos." Again, rivers flow into the sea because evaporation has distributed the sea upon the mountain-tops. The "boundary of the inexpressible" can be expressed only in metaphors.

Barfield now distinguishes logic-as-process, by which a horse is a quadruped, from logic-as-form, by which the quadruped is each individual horse. Essentially he claims that an entity's form or unity is something other than the sum of his parts. To explicate, if we could trace John's every thought or feeling to an appropriate brain-centre or gland, we should not have demonstrated John's wholeness, for this has to be assumed as a preliminary to our investigation.

Although not intended as a conclusion, the existing end of *De Toto* has a ring of finality. After contrasting Form, "which produces unity," with its equally indemonstrable opposite Will, "which produces multiplicity," Barfield says they constitute the poles of an "invisible axis round which the whole cosmos, and in particular the little universe of discourse, revolves." Form, regarded morally and theologically, is "the ever-lasting mercy and forgiveness of God ... with me always, even unto the end of the world." Barfield writes so solemnly of what many would think a mere philosophical conondrum because, as he shows by quoting "If I ascend into Heaven ... and if I go down into Hell, he is there," he is relating the pantheistic "One" or "Whole" to the Christian personal deity. We cannot hope to understand his philosophy without taking down the wall we naturally erect between metaphysical abstractions and living organisms.

Barfield subsequently explained this doctrine of Form more clearly in an essay called "Form in Art and Society."[2] Basing his argument on an article by V. Soloviev,[3] he discusses the "twofold impenetrability" that permits each moment and each body to take over its segment of time and space. The basis of our world is "Being ... dismembered into parts which exclude one another." (Here we recognise "time and space ... threatening to disintegrate me.") Counteracting this divisiveness is an "all-one idea" manifest in organic structure. Even though physical laws operate to maintain the universe in balance, the "fulness of the unitive idea demands that the greatest possible unity of the whole should be realised in the greatest possible independence and freedom of the particular and single elements."

In natural organisms imagination detects the whole-part relationship that in works of art it creates, for "imagination is, precisely, that which experiences form." As in *De Toto*, Barfield maintains that, alike in the cosmos and within every organism, wholeness and partness must co-exist in a state of "paradox, or tension." Love binds into a unity while self-consciousness, "individuation," asserts separateness. The aesthetic or "imaginal" experience conveyed in art depends upon a spiritual discernment of separate strands that are not in normal experience seen separately. Such "separableness," indeed, constitutes the organic property of any work of art. Following Soloviev, Barfield argues, therefore, that the "ideal organic relation" of parts to whole is exemplified in a fugue, wherein the melody recurs in each part. (This recalls his fir-cone example in *De Toto*.)

Barfield now strikes out on his own, arguing that as the organic principle in art originated in Nature, so it now manifests itself socially in the super-session of the hierarchical by the organic society. Presumably this historical insight marks the point of contact between the anthroposophical account of human evolution and the anthroposophical teachings concerning organic agriculture and education.

Barfield brings together issues he and Lewis had debated many years earlier. The establishment of an organic society, he suggests, presupposes a mental climate "wherein the function of imagination in thought will be as self-evident to the effective mass of minds as the function of judgment has been since the epoch of Scholasticism." Inevitably, a judge must be "separate from and set over against the judged." Likewise in "judgmental thought" the thinking subject is "set over against" the object of his thought. This separation, Barfield thinks, might have originated in the Judaic proscription of images, and been sustained in the Christian distinction between Nature and Grace. In any event it culminated in a mechanistic science of which, in his view, Darwinism and behaviourism are the final contortions.

The organicism of Soloviev and Steiner, Barfield maintains, demands for its comprehension a kind of thinking marked as much by imagination as by judgment. What to judgmental thought are "hair-splitting paradoxes"— "dependence which is at the same time independence," "separableness that is inseparable—are "child's play" to the imagination that is accustomed to "sharing, at least in contemplation, the life of nature."

Barfield now more distinctly defines "judgmental" and "imaginal" thought. Citing Kant's definition of judgment as the capacity to think "the particular as contained under the universal," he claims that imaginal thought substitutes "those same tensions or polarities" (the particular and the universal) for the "universals" of judgmental thought. The judging subject affirms his existence in separation from the judged object, but simultaneously represses all thought of its life, and thus "murders to dissect." Both judgmental and imaginal thinking apprehend "unity in multiplicity," but whereas to the judging mind a universal exists as "a static abstraction from the object apprehended," in the imaginative mind a polarity subsists as "a dynamic participation in the process of actual life" manifest in "nature's ordered multiplicity."

"Form in Art and Society" shows conclusively that Lewis and Barfield, though exact contemporaries, lived mentally in different ages. In his "Great War" letters, Lewis ascribed truth to analytic thinking or judgment; to imagination he ascribed meaning, the picturing of a hypothetical entity in the mind, prior to logical proof or disproof of its existence. Characteristically, once he had learned to accord imagination a higher function, he placed it at the apex of an ascending hierarchy.

Each was a Romantic in one of Barfield's two senses—Lewis a lover of the "far away and long ago," Barfield a metaphysician. But Lewis was also an Augustan, a Cartesian rationalist. In his inaugural lecture at Cambridge he ironically called himself "Old Western Man," a product of the printed-book culture of post-Reformation Christian humanism.[4] To him, subject and object necessarily and for ever dwelt apart, the universe remained a hierarchy under God, and if he viewed the ideal Christian society as democratically "leftist," he did so in the belief that sinful men were not to be trusted with absolute power: in fantasy, he hankered after old social hierarchies.

In Barfield's view, a trained imagination could perceive subject and object to be of the same essence, and spiritual hierarchies served that end towards which Creation groans in travail, that all thinking creatures might know themselves as one yet distinct.

Though winning near agreement, Lewis and Barfield never attained it. Conceivably a diagram Barfield made while writing *De Toto*, had he sent it as he intended, might have bridged the narrowing gap. Certainly it brings together all aspects of his thoughts at that time: in philology, grammar, metaphysics and even literary criticism. The reader's patience is asked during the decoding of this at first sight incomprehensible diagram. Barfield's purpose is to represent the relationship between human mental activity as a whole and its various facets. For this reason, he chooses as title the Greek word *Logos*, that connotes grammar, logic, meaning, natural law and the generative principle within mind and body. From the vast number of glosses in Liddell and Scott, the following categories have been selected as most relevant: (i) *relation* (analogy, grammatical rule); (ii) *explanation* (plea,

Grammar	Logic		Exam
λόγος	λόγος		λ ό

Magic power of names etc.

'Holophrase'

(Cognate Accusative)

"   word resembling φυσικο-

δυ...

Attributive Adjective
stage of "conventional
epithet" etc.

λνθε

ὸ 'λνθε

Predicative Adjective. Embryo-Proposition

λνθευ

Subject. Predicate, Copula. Term } born
Proposition } simultaneously

Term
Proposition
and Syllogism }

ὸ 'λν

p.t.o.

ὁ 'λν

ὸ – Σωκ

① See Aristotle Περὶ Ψύχης

λ ό

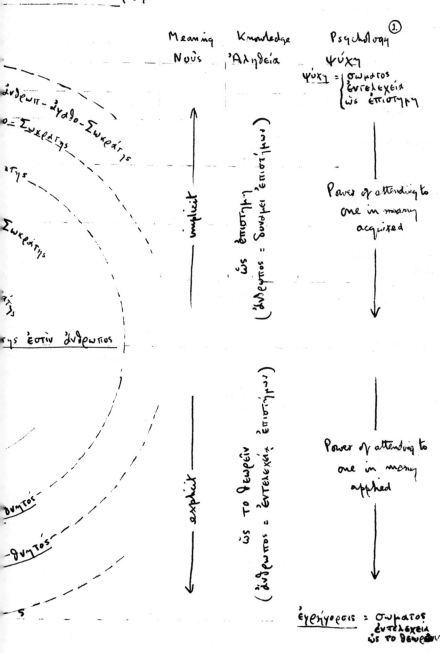

Meaning   Knowledge   Psychology ①

Νοῦς   Ἀλήθεια   Ψύχη

$$ψύχη = \begin{cases} σωματος \\ ἐντελεχεία \\ ὡς ἐπιστήμη \end{cases}$$

ἀνθρωπ- ἀγαθο- Σωκράτης

ο = Σωκράτης

ατης

Σωκράτης

ατης

τ̄ης ἐστιν ἀνθρωπος

implicit

ὡς ἐπιστήμη

(ἀνθρωπος = δυνάμει ἐπιστήμων)

Power of attending to
one in many
acquired

explicit

ὡς το θεωρεῖν

(ἀνθρωπος = ἐντελεχείᾳ ἐπιστήμων)

Power of attending to
one in many
applied

ὁνητός

θνητός

s

ἐγρηγορσις = σωματος
ἐντελεχεία
ὡς το θεωρεῖν

To peri tou logos diagramma
[The diagram about the Logos]

Grammar	Logic
logos	*logos*
[Grammatical relation(s)]	[Term(s) in logic]

Magic power of names, etc.
'Holophrase'

(Cognate accusative)

—do—

Attributive Adjective
stage of "conventional
epithet"

Predicative Adjective	Embryo-Proposition

Subject, Predicate & Copula	Term) born
	Proposition) simultaneously

Term
Proposition
and Syllogism

See Aristotle *Peri Psychē*
[About Soul]

Example   Greek phrases along circular lines
logos
[phrase]

Word resembling   *physiko-zōo-thnēt-anthrōp-agatho-Sōcratēs*
                   [nature- life-mortal-man - good - Socrates]

  ,,   ,,   *thnēt - anthrōp-Sōcratēs*
                     [mortal-man   -Socrates]

  ,,   ,,   *anthrōpo-Sōcratēs*
                     [man   -Socrates]

  ,,   ,,   *ho anthrōp(in)os Sōcratēs*
                     [the   human   Socrates]

  ,,   ,,   *anthrōpos ho Sōcratēs*
                     [the man   Socrates]

  ,,   ,,   *ho Sōcratēs estin anthrōpos*
                     [Socrates is a man]

  ,,   ,,   *ho anthrōpos esti thnētos*
                     [the man   is   mortal]
  ,,   ,,   *ho Sōcratēs esti thnētos*
                     [Socrates is mortal]

Notes   *logos* (at bottom of circles, as at top)

The earliest form of word, the holophrase, is defined in *Poetic Diction* as a "long, rambling conglomeration of sound and meaning." In the diagram, the last three Greek sentences about Socrates are connected by an oval line containing the title "Syllogism," of which they constitute an example.

For convenience, the three columns to the right of the circles are given side-by-side.

Meaning	Knowledge	Psychology
Nous	*Alētheia*	*Psychē*
[Mind]	[True or accurate knowledge]	[Soul]
		psychē = sōmatos *entelecheia* *hōs epistēmē*
		[soul = of body actuality (fulfilment, completion) as (like) knowledge]
Implicit	*hōs epistēmē*	
	[as knowledge]	Power of attending to one in
	(*anthrōpos = dynamei epistēmōn*)	many acquired
	[man understands by means of potentiality (capability)]	
Explicit	*hōs to theōrein*	
	[as (the) to perceive (contemplate)]	Power of attending to one in
		many applied
	(*anthrōpos = entelecheia epistēmōn*)	
	[man = actuality (completion) of understanding]	*Egrēgorsis = sōmatos entelecheia*
		[Awakeness = actuality (fulfilment) of body]

Notes "Implicit" and *hōs ... epistēmōn* are written upright to correspond with the upper halves of the first two columns (down to "Predicative Adjective" and "Embryo-Proposition") and with the upper halves of the circles. "Explicit and *hōs to theōrein* are written upright to correspond with the lower halves of the first three columns, i.e. with the example of a syllogism.

Nous, usually translated "mind," "sense," or "purpose," is used by Plato, Kant and Coleridge to mean pure Reason, human and divine.

Alētheia, literally "not-forgetfulness," i.e. true or accurate memory, is often translated "reality."

Psychē, "soul" or "life," implies "mind" in Aristotle's sense of the operation of mental powers, rather than our modern sense of "emotions-and-imagination."

Entelecheia, often simply rendered as "entelechy," is used by Aristotle to refer to "the static state of fullness or completion," in contrast to *dynamis*, or "potential." *Psychē=sōmatos entelecheia hōs epistēmē* would mean "Soul is the actuality or fulfillment of the body, as knowledge."

Epistēmē, literally "over-standing," may be compared with the English word, "understanding." *Dynamei* is a "dative of means," signifying "by means of which," so that the upper sentence in the "Knowledge" column means "as (or like) understanding, man = (one who) understands by means of potentiality (or capability).

Hōs to theōrein, etc. may be rendered as "Like the act of perceiving (or contemplating), man is (one who) understands (or knows) by means of actuality (or fulfillment, completion)." *Egrēgorsis*, a processive noun, refers rather to coming-awake than being-awake, and Barfield probably implies a coming to full consciousness, as the full realization of the body.

When interpreted line-by-line, the Diagram yields the following sketch of the origin of language and reasoning:

Line 1: Names have a magical power, and the precursor to the sentence is the holophrase, of which Barfield offers an imaginary example that runs together Nature, life, mortal(ity), man, good and Socrates. The processes of thinking and feeling necessarily involve naming, and thereby becoming conscious, of the body.

Lines 2, 3 The next step after forming holophrases is to form the cognate accusative [for example "death," in "to die a hero's death].[5] Barfield's example, in the second circle, combines "mortal," "man" and "Socrates" as necessarily belonging together. This is then refined to 'man-Socrates."

Line 4 Now follows the more limited attributive adjective, as in *ho anthrōp-(in)os Sōcratēs* (the human Socrates). Readers of Homer soon become familiar with conventional epithets, such as *glaukōpis Athēnē* ("flashing-eyed Athene).

Line 5 Words now combine into what Barfield calls "embryo-propositions," (necessitating the use of adjectives as predicates), as in his example *anthrōpos ho Socrates* (literally "man the Socrates"). In this still verbless expression, "man" is divided from Socrates not only by the article but by retaining some of its adjectival quality.

Line 6 Now that grammar has reached the stage of employing an adjective and copula-verb as predicate, reasoning can begin. The sentence at the centre of the circle: *Ho Socrates estin anthropos* ("Socrates is a man"), can be used as the minor premise of the stock syllogism given in the bottom half-circles, viz. *ho anthrōpos esti thnētos* ("man is mortal"); ["Socrates is a man," in centre-line of circles]; *ho Socrates esti thnētos* ("Socrates is mortal").

argument, law or rule of conduct, hypothesis, reason or ground, law of nature, generative principle, Neoplatonic formative forces); (iii) *inward debate* (thinking, reasoning, the faculty of Reason); (iv) *verbal expression* (phrase, discussion, deliberation); (v) *utterance or assertion* (human or divine); (vi) *subject-matter, expression* or *speech* (style, phrase, grammatical term, sentence, language); and (vii) *Word* or *wisdom of God*. No word better exemplifies Barfield's observations on the bifurcative tendency of language.

In the diagram the words on each line in the "Grammar" column correspond to those on the same lines in the "Logic" column and the "Example" circles. The material in the upper and lower half-circles corresponds with that in the upper and lower right-hand columns devoted to Meaning, Knowledge and Psychology.

Before offering an interpretation of the diagram, I shall give a transcript, column by column, with translations in brackets beneath the anglicized Greek phrases, and explanatory notes at the foot of each column. For the reader's convenience, the first two columns are rendered side-by-side.

Next, the mental evolution represented by the growth of grammar and birth of logic is represented in the "Meaning" column as "Implicit" meaning, which becomes "Explicit" once sentence-structure and the syllogism have developed. "Meaning" is related to *Nous* (Mind, Spirit, divine Reason) in that during the dawn of human consciousness man's sensory perceptions had not grown distinct and separate. As in time they focused more distinctly, words and names became more limited and precise in meaning. Barfield represents this focussing process by his narrowing circles. The distinction of subject from object makes possible not only sentence-structure, hence logic, but also explicit statement and conscious knowledge, as distinct from the implicit knowledge available through sensory perception.[6] Parallel with this linguistic development, the mind, always capable of sensing the oneness behind diverse appearances, learns to express consciously the distinctions between the One and the Many, between immortal and mortal, and to draw the inference concerning Socrates, having once focused itself upon him.

In this "Diagram about the Logos" Barfield relates grammatical evolution to the growth of human reasoning and consciousness. As he acknowledges, in the bottom left-hand corner, his psychology harks back to Aristotle's *Peri Psychē (De Anima)*. While his reading of the evolutionary process depends on his adapting from Coleridge and Steiner a definition of evolution as a creature's fulfilment of its potential, rather than its transmutation into another species, it has some unique features.[7] Primarily it is unique in that Barfield draws his evidence not from fossils or artefacts but from language, that human acquisition most evidently expressing man's "enjoyment" of his

112

inner life and "contemplation" of the world about him. Like the early theologians, the Neoplatonists and the Scholastics, he traces words to "the Word," that is the Logos. As the human mind stems from the divine, so man's primary imagination wordlessly combines the elements in man's environment, and his secondary imagination, together with the power of reasoning, are outgrowths from the universal Mind or *Nous* (Reason). (Hence Steiner's philosophy is often called "noetic.") That very self-consciousness whose growth Barfield has traced in philology, literary theory and philosophy he would, like Coleridge before him, regard as evidence of the "eternal act of creation in the infinite I AM."[8]

PART FOUR:

THE "GREAT WAR" —
BEFORE AND AFTER

CHAPTER 11

Peace

Even shooting wars rarely end in total victory or defeat, nor does peace arrive suddenly. The war of words tends to die away as anger gives place to boredom. What is astonishing about the friendly "Great War" between Lewis and Barfield is not that it sputtered out but that it lasted so long and nurtured so many ideas later developed in published works. In the end, by leaving their final manuscripts unfinished, both combatants walked away from the field.[1]

All that visibly remains of their five-year-long conflict is an incomplete and disorderly pile of letters, followed by a few essays and disputations too erudite for easy reading and in any case inconclusive. Yet the combat originated in part from a thesis that marked a new turning in poetic theory, while its after-effects included the shaping of Lewis's impressive and widely influential body of critical and creative writing, as well as Barfield's increasingly attractive blend of philology and metaphysics. As already shown, the disputants brought to bear a formidable range of philosophical equipment: a mutual understanding of Plato and Aristotle, Lewis's grasp of Aquinas and Kant, Barfield's of the Neoplatonists, and a considerable though by no means comprehensive knowledge of modern philosophy. Neither, for example, seemed aware of twentieth century empiricism in the works of Russell and G. E. Moore, of Marxian or scientific positivism, of evolutionary biological theory or recent work in physics.

What use did each of them make of this armoury?

A medieval philosopher miraculously enabled to read these manuscripts would have partially understood them as disputations between a nominalist and a realist, both heretical. His report might have run thus:

Under the influence of Plato, the blessed Thomas Aquinas and an unknown moralist named Kant, Lewis, a nominalist, maintains the separateness of his inner world of ideas from the outer realm of Nature, and urges Barfield for his soul's health to accept the world's reality but deny its values. By what agency Lewis has been seduced into forsaking our religion for a "Spirit" remains for the inquisitors to determine, but the conclusions he draws from such blameless premises furnish evidence that his reason has been corrupted by the devils whose existence he denies.

The realist, Barfield, upholds the existence of God and the celestial hierarchies, and especially the dependence of both Nature and human reason upon the divine Word, but scandalously identifies virtue with that self-awareness any Christian must renounce. This also is a matter for the inquisitors, yet Barfield ought first to be called to defend his interesting notion concerning the antagonism of matter and form.

From our end of the telescope, Lewis appears to typify the post-medieval sundering of man from the observed world. Because he tended to think analytically, so to speak "judgmentally," he proved an ideal critic for Barfield. The young Lewis we encounter in these disputations, however, seems destined not only for eminence but for a kind of tragedy. Throwing himself into the medieval scholastic game with more zest and expertise than Barfield, he shows both more rigour and more exuberance. Even so, unease appears not only in what I have dubbed his "existential anxiety" but in his moral role-playing, his assumed *contemptus mundi*. His eventual acceptance of Christian belief appears logical, even inevitable.

What does not appear inevitable is Lewis's ultimate combination of a rationalism and world-view pertaining to the medieval ages of faith with a philosophical position characteristic of British empiricists from Locke to Russell, one in which subject and object are sharply distinguished. Lewis came to think of God, angels, man and animals in the hierarchy envisaged by theologians from St. Paul to Aquinas and to depict man's being and destiny within the framework of Pauline and Augustinian eschatology. Only late in his career, however, does Lewis, one of the ablest logicians among modern apologists, probe the terms of logic itself. In all his religious and critical writing, he attends scrupulously to the meanings of terms, but either looks backward to meanings established at fixed points in the past, or else insists that present meanings alone shall receive attention.[2] *Studies in Words* marks a new but belated departure, perhaps under the influence of Barfield but more probably under that of Lewis's new colleagues at Cambridge.

Like Kant, Johnson, or Jane Austen, Lewis identifies Christian morality with a stoical fulfilment of duty. The Freudian questioning of that morality, especially of conscience (the super-ego), he mentions only to condemn. Rarely does he discuss the implications of biological and social evolution, or modern concepts regarding the nature of matter. To call Lewis "old-world" is both to echo his own humorous self-description and to indulge in "chronological snobbery." From his vast accumulation of books and essays, however, it really does appear not only that novelists and poets since the early Yeats have added little to our literary heritage, but that, in all the great outpouring of philosophy, and psychology since Kant, only those studies, such as Jung's on mythology, that bear on Lewis's special interests, are to be esteemed as fundamental additions to man's understanding of himself and his environment.

In the short term, Lewis has exerted an immense influence upon readers without and within the academic world. In so far as he instilled respect for orderly and coherent argument, vitality of expression and the re-examination of beliefs assumed on the basis of their modernity rather than their cogency, his influence was wholly benign. In retrospect, however, his apologetic activity has an element of tragic failure. He wrote what he honestly thought true, out-reasoning most of those that chose to argue with him, and no controversialist can do more. Yet one of the sharpest intellects of the day employed itself in justifying convictions that seem to afford little scope to the enquiring and creative mind. However true the beliefs, however sound the ethic, however lucid and compelling the prose, the total effect of Lewis's religious books and essays is to direct attention away from all that has proved most vital in the intellectual life of the past two centuries, as much from the nineteenth-century debate over evolution as from the modern ones over existentialism, linguistic analysis and behaviourist psychology. He asks his reader to rest content in the beliefs and formulations that would have satisfied say, Isaac Watts or Jane Austen. Even the tremendous accumulation of New Testament criticism over the past two centuries is bypassed with the *a priori*, even perhaps "bulverist" argument that the critics approach the sacred texts with erroneous modern assumptions.[3] For a generation Lewis defended, even partially repopulated, a city set upon an eroded cliff, when it needed to be rebuilt upon sounder ground. Already the very activity of apologetic writing to which he devoted himself most unselfishly and which brought him both fame and academic disfavour, as well as a crushing burden of correspondence, begins to look dated. As Barfield early foresaw, the old mode of theological argumentation, like the old order in society, could not but yield to time and change. Lewis used his mind and art, and produced some of the most effortless argumentative prose in the language, to defend a *status quo* that appears indefensible.

Lest this judgment be mistaken for advocacy of that vague ethical liberalism so exasperating to Lewis, let me express a conviction that the traditional "scheme of salvation" and once-for-all discontinuous and exclusive revelation are unlikely to regain their power over the heart of Western man. The Christian religion can only re-establish itself in a pagan society by conveying and extending the religious experience of countless devotees, past and present. By "experience of devotees" I mean primarily the mystical tradition, the *philosophia perennis*, stemming from pseudo-Dionysius, Eckhart, St.

Catherine, Ruysbroek, St. John of the Cross, Boehme and their successors down to Blake and Yeats, but also the Hindu, Buddhist and Sufi mysticism with which it has so much in common. Undoubtedly Lewis read with deep interest many of the mystical writings concerned, but the core of his teaching remained the Pauline and Augustinian scheme of salvation. It seems to me that the convergence of mystical traditions in our time, and the search for a new formulation of the Christian faith, with or without images, reflects a continuing process of religious experience and response, while Lewis's theology remains essentially static, a case, theologically speaking, of arrested development.

Christian experience cannot forever be confined within the thought-forms either of the schoolmen or the post-Reformation logicians. Indeed, Christianity is not tied to any *Zeitgeist* or conventional mode of reasoning. As Lewis himself implies in his *Summa*, the divine presence and absence cannot be contemplated but only enjoyed. Traditional images of Heaven and Hell, like traditional credal formulations, represent human contemplation of the divine at given points in history.

At a sub-conscious level, Lewis was deeply influenced by Barfield. Though he had ridiculed the latter's belief in supernatural "intermediaries," their existence is a cardinal assumption in the space trilogy. Indeed, the planetary *That Hideous Strength* features just such a demonic conspiracy as Lewis had ridiculed in a "Great War" letter. By the dawn of the atomic age, Lewis's manipulators and empire-builders, however, were not financiers but scientists.

Moreover, if his planetary beings were conceived (like the conspiracy in *That Hideous Strength*) under influence from the tales read by Tolkien and Charles Williams to their fellow-Inklings, the action in both *Perelandra* and the "Narnia" stories presupposes abolition of the barrier between conscious and inanimate forms of existence. In *The Lion, the Witch and the Wardrobe*, for example, climate and landscape change according to whether the good or the evil power has the upper hand. Subject and object undoubtedly remained distinct at a rational level, but the gap was bridged in Lewis's fantasies. That Narnia's fauns, dryads and talking beasts were derived from classical and medieval literature does not affect the argument, for Barfield ascribes myth itself, their ultimate source, to a "primal participation" phase recapitulated in childhood. During this phase, supposedly, man neither experienced a sense of separation from Nature nor learned to distinguish natural from supernatural.

The "Narnia" stories have generally been adjudged artistically more successful than the planetary romances. As in weaving them Lewis liberated the child subsisting within his own personality, so they continue to prove immensely attractive to children. Their enchantment mainly consists not in their obvious fairy-tale and theological elements of magic and the conflict of good and evil, but in their embodiment of the child's primal awareness of reality as indivisible. While resisting any impulse to offend the author's spirit by practising posthumous psycho-analysis, I would suggest that in the Narnia series he usually preserved an equipoise between this childlike unitive consciousness and the parent-like, super-ego religious feeling that prepossessed him in favour of God as Father rather than Son. (This balance may account for the large adult readership the tales enjoy.)

In the planetary romances, maintaining the more delicate balance between these two elements and the realism of the ego or adult consciousness proved beyond Lewis's creative gift. *That Hideous Strength* is the weakest novel in the series because its "normal" adult characters are inadequate to bear the weight of meaning assigned them, just as in the Narnia books the stereotyped London cabbies and other real-life characters carry less conviction than either the children or the animal and supernatural characters. Significantly some adult characters, such as Weston in *That Hideous Strength*, have been identified with actual figures, but the child characters exist in their own right, within the forms of the appropriate stories.

Inevitably time and subsequent scholarship will obscure, though not obliterate, the major figures in twentieth-century academic criticism, of whom on any supposition Lewis must be adjudged one. This is not the place in which to assess his critical and scholarly attainment in *The Allegory of Love* or *English Literature of the Sixteenth Century, Excluding Drama*, but I hope to have shown how, by enlarging his historical, critical and psychological perspectives, the arguments with Barfield made that achievement possible.

Lewis's view of literature differed most fundamentally from that of Dr Leavis, his rival for pre-eminence on the British academic scene, in that Lewis treated reading as a form of exploration in which "one thing leads to another,"[4] while Leavisite critics treat literature as a real and earnest pursuit whose end is to express and produce an awareness of life proper to sensitive and responsible adults. Lewis identified literature with active or participatory reading[5] while Leavisites have often identified it with approved books and authors. He viewed literature as man's highest, most spiritual form of play, while they view it as a form of education in morally responsible living, a role he would assign to religion. His enjoyment was child-like, subject-centred, fundamentally religious; theirs is adult, object-centred, fundamentally secular.

As any reader must by now realise, Barfield, at the time of the "Great War," lacked Lewis's expertise in formal logic, his breadth of reading, above all his wit and liveliness in expression. Nor for all his efforts has he blossomed as a creative writer. It is with trepidation, therefore, that I express the belief that though Barfield's books—*History in English Words, Poetic Diction, Saving the Appearances, Worlds Apart, Speaker's Meaning, What Coleridge Thought* and the essays printed in *Romanticism Comes of Age* and *The Rediscovery of Meaning*—will never attract so wide a readership as the far more numerous books by Lewis, they will be read longer and to more profound effect. Even in Barfield's "juvenilia" (his own term for the "Great War" papers), he questions common assumptions about human nature and experience in a way his opponent does not. Lewis directs his most penetrating questions at Barfield's thesis rather than at life and consciousness themselves. In the end, the *Summa* is a compound of naïve moral attitude, of game and of philosophical terms derived from elsewhere but never fully exploited or of undeveloped concepts (such as "imagination as supreme mode of spiritual experience"). It is Barfield who asks how enjoying subject differs from contemplated object, or who traces the path taken by meaning from perceived reality through imagination to conscious formulation. Fortunate as he was to have his earliest, perhaps most original speculations criticised with such incisive common-sense, even his unfinished *De Toto* has bore more fruit subsequently than anything Lewis wrote in the controversies. More than once, indeed, Lewis seems to realise that Barfield's mind has the greater potential. His consistent treatment of Barfield as at least his intellectual equal argues unusual modesty and discernment in a distinguished scholar considering the ideas of a friend outside academic life.

That Barfield's thought is both more original and more profound I have come to believe while studying these controversies. From reading *Poetic Diction*, their starting-point and *Romanticism Comes of Age*, their immediate successor, and the later works that were their ultimate consequence, I have come to think him the more important figure, if a philosopher and critical theorist be judged according to his capacity to show how contemporary thought-forms and reactions to man's inner and external worlds differ from those characteristic of former ages and how they manifest a universal human identity.

I say this in the full awareness that *The Allegory of Love*, to instance but a single work of Lewis, was an epoch-making piece of historical criticism. Nevertheless, its awareness of the medieval world-view and many of its insights have been digested, or in some instances rejected, by younger literary scholars. In the nature of things, even critical books that open new fields lose their impact. Indeed, within a few generations the Narnia chronicles may well be the only books by Lewis that continue to be widely read, as distinct from being recorded with respect, and studied by literary scholars.

Poetic Diction, however, provokes the reader to think about poetry and its relation to the cosmos, and Barfield's subsequent works provoke thought about the human psyche, in ways extending far beyond the scope of literary history. Future students of twentieth-century thought may well find Barfield —like Einstein or Popper in scientific theory, or Bonhoeffer in theology— among the diagnosticians of a profound change in human consciousness, one comparable to the Reformation or Enlightenment. That change is in a sense an anti-Enlightenment, in that it involves regarding man not as the sole rational being in a sub-rational Nature, but as an already self-conscious being learning to extend that self-consciousness so as to communicate with and benignantly participate in a natural order that in his arrogance, turbulent passions and mistaken philosophical assumptions he has all but destroyed.

I hasten to disclaim the inference that the figures mentioned represent any kind of consensus or common front. What Barfield does seem to have in common with Einstein, Popper, Bonhoeffer and for that matter De Chardin is a certain tentativeness, a sense that truth lies not in "facts" that once discovered remain as certainties, but in a continuous reaching into the unknown or re-consideration of experience. They would all see the process of discovery as an exercise of imagination, in the sense Barfield specifies in a "Great War" letter. Inevitably Lewis's writing, on theology in particular, is an effort not of creative Reason but of Understanding, that looks backward over the path traced by earlier scholars.

Since even a dead religion, such as the Greek mythological cults, can continue to furnish material for literary or artistic creation, the foregoing strictures can apply only within the realms of philosophy and theology. The novels of Tolkien, Lewis himself and to a lesser extent Charles Williams bear witness to the continuing power of the traditional Christian beliefs to inspire literary creation.

Within the confines of this study of Lewis's formative arguments with Barfield, any judgment of their relative importance would necessarily remain a matter of assertion. Indeed, it would be foolish to set up an unreal competition between two authors who have far more important areas of agreement than of difference.[6] Neither, for example, could have conducted this fundamentally friendly controversy with, say, Bertrand Russell or A. J. Ayer. The reader must confirm or deny my estimate through his own study of the principal works of Lewis and Barfield.

Should future historians perceive the change of human consciousness described above, they may well see Barfield as one who helped bring about a re-unification of our fragmented culture by ensuring both that the role of imagination in scientific and historical enquiry receive its due recognition, and that poetry, drama and fiction, as well as religion, again become means by which men create or modify themselves and so re-form their environment.

NOTES

1 Paper "Bluspels and Flalansferes" given 1936, in *Rehabilitations and Other Essays* (London, 1939), pp. 133-58. See also Lewis's essay "Historicism" (1950), reprinted in *Christian Reflections*, ed. W. Hooper (Grand Rapids, 1967), pp. 100-13.

2 Undated letter, apparently a testimonial, in Wade Collection.

3 C. S. Lewis, *Surprised by Joy: The Shape of My Early Life* (London, 1955), p. 196.

4 As Lewis lectured from notes, *The Discarded Image: An Introduction to Medieval and Renaissance Literature* (Cambridge, 1964) merely approximates to the "Prolegomena."

5 Letter to Arthur Greeves, 2 June, 1930, No. 113 in Wade Collection.

6 Roger Lancelyn Green and Walter Hooper, *C. S. Lewis* (London, 1974), pp. 67-79.

7 Subsequently co-editor of the *Anthroposophical Quarterly*, Harwood taught at a Rudolf Steiner school near Oxford and accompanied Lewis and Barfield on the walking-tour mentioned herein.

8 Entry in Lewis's journal dated 7 July 1923, cited in Amos Franceschelli, "The Teachings of Rudolf Steiner with Special Reference to C. S. Lewis": *Bulletin of New York C. S. Lewis Society* No. 43 (May 1973), 2-6.

9 Poem entitled "Fidelia Vulnera Amantes" under note "Please keep this and return when you next return the Summa. It is the best I can do at present. (I mean the tractate, not the sonnet!)" Above Belfast address, Lewis hints at early departure, hence date probably late summer, 1929.

10 Lewis, *Surprised by Joy*, p. 189.

11 Lewis, letter to Barfield, 24 January 1926, in Wade Collection.

12 Rudolf Steiner, *The Philosophy of Freedom*, trans. M. Wilson (London, 1964), pp. 217-18. (Barfield used a 1918 translation, *The Philosophy of Spiritual Activity*.)

13 Lewis, letter to Barfield, 28 February 1936, in Wade Collection.

14 Barfield, "From East to West," (1929), in his *Romanticism Comes of Age* (London, 1944; New York, 1966), pp. 25-26. This and later references are to 1966 edition.

[15] Lewis, letters to Greeves, 1915-16, in Wade Collection: No. 6, on pleasures of Irish mythology; No. 8 on Morris romances; No. 9 on "romantic strangeness you and I like" in Coleridge's "Christabel"; Nos. 10, 12 on Malory; No. 16 on *Volsung Saga.* Cf. with No. 37 "I believe in no religion," Christianity a superstition, yet *Kalevala* praised as "not tame ... but full of primeval spirits, floods, magic and talking beasts" and No. 38 on "tomfoolery" of Virgin Birth and "magic healings," regret Greeves not liberated from "beliefs that always considerably lessened my happiness." In No. 39, Lewis praises "fey" exaltation when dreaming and approves Scott and Maeterlinck.

[16] But R. J. Reilly, *Romantic Religion* (Athens, Ga., 1971), p. 7f., likens Barfield to Coleridge, Lewis to Shelley and Charles Williams to Wordsworth.

[17] Barfield, "Either-Or," in C. A. Huttar (comp.), *Imagination and the Spirit: Essays ... Presented to Clyde A. Kilby* (Grand Rapids, 1971), pp. 25-42. Concept derived from Coleridge.

[18] Samuel Alexander, *Space, Time and Deity* (London, 1920), I 12 ff.

[19] Barfield, *Poetic Diction*, 3rd edn. (Middletown, 1973), p. 103 ff.

[20] Lewis, *Surprised by Joy*, p. 189.

[21] ———, *Studies in Words* (Cambridge, 1960, rpt. 1967), pp. 191-96.

[22] Barfield, "C. S. Lewis and Historicism," in *Bulletin of New York C. S. Lewis Society*, No. 43 (August, 1975), 3-9.

[23] Lewis, *The Case for Christianity* (London, 1964, rpt. from *Broadcast Talks*, London, 1942), pp. 43-44.

[24] ———, *Preface to "Paradise Lost"* (London, 1942), p. 61 ff.

[25] Barfield, *op. cit.*, 7 n.

[26] *Surprised by Joy*, pp. 130-33.

[27] Lewis, "What Chaucer really did to 'Il Filostrato'," *Essays and Studies*, XVIII (1932), 56-75.

[28] Imparted to me in conversation by Mr Colin Hardie, Fellow of Magdalen College.

[29] Letter to Greeves, 21 December 1929 (No. 108 in Wade Collection).

[30] In *Times Literary Supplement*, 13 January 1927, p. 27.

[31] Copied and sent to console Greeves for rejection of book, 18 August 1930 (No. 133 in Wade Collection).

[32] *Poetic Diction* review: *Times Literary Supplement*, 17 May 1928, p. 375. *History in English Words* -do-: *Saturday Review*, 23 January 1926, p. 95; *Booklist* (Chicago) XXIII (November 1926), 64; *Boston Transcript*, 4 September 1926, p. 4; *Literary Review* (New York), 11 September 1926, p. 13; *New Statesman* XXVI (1926), 23 January, p. 450.

CHAPTER 2

[1] Barfield, *Poetic Diction*, pp. 65-66, 73-74, 79-81.

[2] *Ibid.*, p. 92.

[3] *Ibid.*, Ch. VII, *passim*.

[4] *Ibid.*, pp. 62-63.

[5] *Ibid.*, p. 181.

[6] *Ibid.*, p. 184.

[7] *Ibid.*, pp. 136-38.

[8] *Ibid.*, p. 140.

[9] From Coleridge, *Biographia Literaria*, Ch. XIII, in Shedd, (ed.) *Complete Works of Samuel Taylor Coleridge* (New York, 1868), III 364.

> Grant me a nature having two contrary forces, the one of which tends to expand indefinitely, while the other strives to apprehend or *find* itself in this infinity, and I will cause the whole world of intelligences with the whole system of their representations to rise up before you.

[10] From Aristotle, *De Anima* 430a 10-25 (Bk. III, Ch. V), in translation by Sir David Ross (dual-language edition, London, 1961), Barfield's chosen extracts run:

> And there is an intellect which is of this kind by becoming all things, and there is another which is so by producing all things. . . . And this intellect is distinct, unaffected and unmixed, being in essence activity. . . . Actual knowledge is identical with its object. . . . (But we do not remember because this is unaffected, whereas the passive intellect is perishable), and without this thinks nothing.

Barfield thus relates Aristotle's distinction of active from passive reason to Coleridge's concept of a polarity within nature and the human mind.

[11] Cf. Plato, *Theaetatus* and *Timaeus* with Barfield, *Poetic Diction*, p. 203: "early Greek philosophy . . . is now known to have been actually an inquiry into the nature of knowledge, although *it thought itself to be* an inquiry into the nature of *Being*." For contemporary and earlier interpretations of *Timaeus*, see A. E. Taylor, *A Commentary on Plato's "Timaeus"* (London, 1928).

[12] Plato, *Theatatus*, 186B.

[13] Plato, *Timaeus*, 44d, 71b.

[14] Cf., Barfield, *History in English Words* (London, 1926, rpt. Grand Rapids, 1967), pp. 169-70: "The consciousness of 'myself' and the distinction between 'myself' . . . all other selves . . . and the external world . . . is quite a recent achievement of the human spirit"; with Barfield, *What Coleridge Thought* (Middletown, 1971), p. 76: " . . . the life of nature is at all levels a power of 'separative projection', and separative projection ('the eternal act of creation') is what the act of self-consciousness—what the act of imagination—is."

[15] Aristotle, *De Anima*, 417a 12, 431 b 25-30.

[16] Aristotle, *Metaphysics*, 10, 70a 1-5; *Physics*, 193b.

[17] My comment refers to communication and learning. Re process of discovery, my colleague Dr E.-H. Kluge informs me of anticipations of atomic theory in Lucretius' *De Rerum Natura* and Kekulés dream of carbon and hydrogen atoms dancing, that suggested his representation of benzene ring.

[18] Teilhard de Chardin, *Le Phenomène Humain*, VI^ed. (Paris, 1955), I 50 ff. ("Existence").

[19] Rudolf Steiner, *An Outline of Occult Science*, trans. M. and H. B. Mongès (New York, 1972), p. 23.

[20] S. T. Coleridge, *Biographia Literaria* Ch. IV (Shedd 3.201-02) ; Ch. XIII.

[21] Barfield, *Romanticism Comes of Age*, p. 17.

[22] E.g. A. Owen Barfield, Introduction to *The Case for Anthroposophy: Selections from "Von Seelenrätseln" by Rudolf Steiner* (London, 1970) ; A. P. Shepherd, *A Scientist of the Invisible* (London, 1954) ; Michael Wilson, Introduction to Steiner, *The Philosophy of Freedom*, trans. Wilson. See also Epilogue to Steiner, *The Redemption of Thinking: A Study in the Philosophy of Thomas Aquinas*, trans. and ed. A. P. Shepherd and Mildred Robertson Nicoll (London, 1956), pp. 116-54.

[23] Shepherd, *Scientist of the Invisible*, pp. 40-41.

[24] Steiner, *Philosophy of Freedom*, p. 143.

[25] Shepherd, *Scientist of the Invisible*, p. 71.

[26] Franceschelli, "Anthroposophy . . . Lewis," 5.

[27] Steiner, *Occult Science*, p. 35.

[28] ———, *Philosophy of Freedom*, p. 14, 19. Cf. Barfield's distinction in *Speaker's Meaning* (Middletown, 1967) between language as expression and as communication, and theory of original and final participation in *Saving the Appearances* (London, 1957).

[29] Steiner, *Knowledge of Higher Worlds*, p. 119.

[30] *Ibid.*, pp. 80-93. (Cf. successive deaths in T. S. Eliot's *Waste Land.*)

[31] *Ibid.*, p. 221-28.

[32] *Ibid.*, p. 211-12.

[33] For explanation of Fall as regression, see Steiner, *St. John's in Relation to Other Gospels*, trans. G. Metaxa (London, 1933) pp. 59-63; on *Agapē* contrasted with Darwinian struggle for existence, see *ibid.*, pp. 26, 140, and contrasted with kinship ties, see Steiner, *St. John's Gospel*, Trans. M. B. Monges (New York, 1962), p. 75ff.

[34] ———, *Occult Science* pp. 101, 109-18, 374-76.

[35] Explained in Barfield, *Romanticism Comes of Age*, pp. 101, 107 ff., and Steiner, *Occult Science*, p. 357.

[36] Unlike Freud, Steiner uses "Ego" to denote self-consciousness only. For discussion, see his *St. Matthew's Gospel*, trans. H. Collison (London, n.d.) Lecture VII; *St. John's Gospel*, Lecture X; *St. John's in Relation*, Lecture VI.

[37] Especially Shepherd, *Scientist of the Invisible*; Steiner, *Occult Science*; *Art in the Light of Mystery-Wisdom*, trans. J. Collis (London, 1970); *The Essentials of Education*, trans. H. Collison (London, 1926), and *The Roots of Education*, trans. Helen Fox (London, 1968).

[38] Explained in Steiner, *St. John's in Relation*, pp. 19-21:

> Everything that happens in the physical-sense world has its counterpart in the spirit-world. . . . Whereas the ocular, sensible impression of the hand passes away, its spiritual counterpart remains engraved in the spirit-world. . . . So that, when our spiritual eyes are opened, we can follow the trace and find the spiritual counterpart of everything that has happened in the world.

For reprinted articles on "Akashic chronicle" of pre-history, see Steiner, *Cosmic Memory* (New York, 1959).

[39] Karl Popper, *The Logic of Scientific Discovery* (London, 1958) pp. 46-47.

[40] I Corinthians xv. 17.

[41] Lewis, *The Discarded Image* (rpt. 1967), p. 11.

[42] M. H. Abrams, *Natural Supernaturalism* (New York, 1971), pp. 313-16.

[43] For fuller account, see Dorothy Emmet's Preface to Alexander, *Space, Time and Deity* (2nd ed., 1966).

[44] In essay on "Historicism," *loc. cit.*

[45] Lewis, *Surprised by Joy*, p. 206: "I accepted this distinction at once and have ever since regarded it as an indispensable tool of thought."

[46] Cf. Alexander, *Space, Time and Deity*, ii 89: "A mind which broods over itself in dangerous practical introspection abandons itself to the enjoyment of itself . . . ," with St. Augustine *Of Free-will*, trans. J. H. S. Burleigh (London: *Library of Christian Classics*, vol. vi, 1953), p. 216: "if the mind, being immediately conscious of itself, takes pleasure in itself . . . the greater it wants to be the less it becomes."

[47] E.g. Alexander, *Space, Time and Deity*, ii 292. Cf. also Steiner, *Christianity as Mystical Fact*, trans. anon 2nd ed. (New York, 1972), p. 138; and statement that Hamlet had real existence, in—*St. Mark's Gospel*, trans. E. McArthur (New York, 1950), p. 13.

[48] Alexander, *Space, Time and Deity*, I 134, 161.

[49] Specifically: (1) moral law based on reason, not divine fiat, Kant, *Critique of Practical Reason*, trans. Thomas Kingsmill Abbott, 6th ed. (London, 1909), pp. 260-61, 282; (2) duties to be performed out of free-will, not hope or fear of reward or punishment, *ibid.*, p. 226; (3) a rational nature exists as an end in itself, *The Moral Law: Kant's*

"Groundwork of Metaphysics and Morals", trans. H. J. Paton (London, 1948, rpt. New York, 1964), pp. 62-64; (4) the categorical imperative, *ibid.*, pp. 88-89. Lewis goes beyond Kant by saying sanctions rob an act of value.

[50] Objections and rejoinders are standard features of an Aquinas treatise. With Lewis, *De Bono et Malo*, cf. Aquinas, *De Malo*.

[51] See F. C. Copleston, *Aquinas* (London, 1955), p. 66, with Aquinas, *Summa Theologica*, Ia, 16, 2, cited in Copleston, p. 177.

[52] Aquinas, *op. cit.*, Ia, 5, 48, 3, cited in Copleston, pp. 144-45.

[53] Croce's *Estetica come scienza* (Bari, 1917) is Vol. I of his *Filosofia come scienza dello spirito*. His article "Aesthetics," in *Encyclopedia Britannica*, 14th ed. (London, 1929-30), has the gist of his aesthetic theory. Dr. Dorothy Emmet recalls Professor J. A. Smith, of Madgalen College, Oxford, as an especially keen oral exponent.

[54] Croce, "Aesthetics," *loc. cit.*, 264: "Hence poetry must be called neither feeling, nor image ... but 'contemplation of feeling' or 'lyrical intuition' or (... the same thing) 'pure intuition' [free from] all historical and critical reference to the reality or unreality of the images of which it is woven, and apprehending the pure throb of life in its ideality."

[55] Croce, "Aesthetics," *loc. cit.*, 264-65.

[56] *Urphänomene*, in Goethe's sense: phenomena fundamental to any intellectual process, e.g., for science of Optics, Light. On Goethe's *Urpolaritat* (primal polarity) between original antithetical realities, e.g. Light and Darkness, see Rudolf Magnus, *Goethe as a Scientist*, trans. Heinz Norden (New York 1949, rpt. 1961), pp. 171-73.

[57] Kant, *Critique of Pure Reason*, trans. Norman Kemp Smith (London, 1964), pp. 74, 87.

[58] Letter to Dr Clyde S. Kilby, in Wade Collection.

[59] Augustine, *Confessions*, VIII v 7; VIII i 2.

[60] *Ibid.*, VIII x 16;—*City of God*, cited in N. F. Cantor and P. L. Klein, *Augustine and St. Thomas Aquinas* (Waltham, Mass., 1969), pp. 55-56.

[61] Cited in Copleston, p. 94.

[62] Barfield, *History in English Words*, pp. 113-14.

CHAPTER 3

[1] Mr Barfield comments that this letter "did not come first in time" but may usefully be treated first.

[2] A London suburb. On *hoti*, see O.E.D. entry.

[3] Perranporth, Cornwall, September, 1929. See Green and Hooper, *C. S. Lewis*, p. 92.

[4] Lewis cites "the Poet ... nothing affirmeth," from "Defence of Poesie," in A. Feuillerat (ed.): *Prose Works of Sir Philip Sidney* (Cambridge, 1912, rpt. 1962), III 29.

[5] Summer, 1927. See Green and Hooper, *C. S. Lewis*, p. 92. On Lewis's need to believe in an external reality, Mr Barfield comments: "I have reason to believe that is a very true statement about C.S.L., though I am not sure how far, if at all, he himself was aware of it."

[6] 1928 edition dedicated to "Clive Hamilton," subsequent ones to Lewis by name.

[7] "Bulverism," a Socratic Society paper reprinted in C. S. Lewis, *God in the Dock: Essays on Theology and Ethics*, ed. Walter Hooper (Grand Rapids, 1970), pp. 271-77.

[8] Barfield's argument, "What if Ahriman wished to deceive us? Would he not wish us to think ... ?" was parodied by Lewis as "What if Gyges were present ... wearing his ring [of invisibility]?" See Plato, *Republic*, ii 359 d.

[9] In a letter to Greeves, Lewis complains that a "Papist" Irish publisher reprinting his *Pilgrim's Regress* wishes to represent its argument as a Catholic's attack upon "my own country" (December 1935: No. 179 in Wade Collection.) Nevertheless, Tolkien, a Roman Catholic, had for many years been a close friend.

CHAPTER 4

[1] Letter to Dr C. S. Kilby, in Wade Collection. On kinds of disputation, see Introduction to Copleston, *Aquinas*.

[2] Reproduced in Maurice Hussey, *Chaucer's World* (Cambridge, 1967).

[3] Diary entry quoted in Green and Hooper, *C. S. Lewis*, p. 91.

[4] As far as *Summa* II iii only.

[5] Barfield and Steiner also use the Greek noun *Nous* and derivative "noetic" as synonyms for "Spirit" and "spiritual." Neoplatonic texts, especially by Plotinus, use *Nous* to mean a divine world of ideas prior to creation, cf. Coleridge's "Ideas of Reason."

[6] Re-formulated in Lewis, *The Problem of Pain* (London, 1940), p. 18.

[7] Steiner, *Occult Science*, pp. 25-29.

[8] For a more orthodox view, see Lewis, *Preface to "Paradise Lost"*, pp. 65, 68.

[9] A central theme of George Macdonald's *Lilith*, explicated by Lewis to Greeves, Letter 171 (1 September 1933) in Wade Collection.

[10] Lewis and E. M. W. Tillyard, *The Personal Heresy: A Controversy* (London, 1939).

[11] Steiner, *Philosophy of Freedom*, Ch. 1, *passim*; pp. 133-35.

[12] Lewis cites Santayana, presumably "Platonism and the Spiritual Life" in *Works of George Santayana* (New York, 1936), X 186.

CHAPTER 5

[1] A word much used by Alexander, whose work Mr Barfield says he had not read. Lewis, however, had told him of the Contemplation-Enjoyment passage as illuminating an experience Barfield was trying to describe.

[2] On this "white occultism" see Steiner, *Knowledge of Higher Worlds*, p. 258.

[3] Cf. Goethe, cited in Magnus, *Goethe as Scientist*, p. 170: "Hypotheses are like the scaffolding in front of a building, to be dismantled when the building is completed. To the worker the scaffolding is indispensable, but he must not confuse it with the building itself." Lewis criticises Barfield's metaphor in similar terms.

[4] The etymology of *logos* given in Liddell and Scott conveys no suggestion of "mineral metaphor." Barfield probably means "proper to the mineral world," i.e. belonging to a lower order of activity (Dr Whalley's suggestion).

[5] Barfield, "Either-Or" essay.

[6] Barfield, letter to L. Adey, 1977 (mislaid).

[7] In essay "Either-Or."

[8] Cf. "Christian *energeia*" in Barfield, *What Coleridge Thought* p. 8f.

CHAPTER 6

[1] Cf. Lewis's criticisms of ethical relativism in *Mere Christianity* (London, 1952), Ch. 1; *The Abolition of Man* (London, 1943), Chs. 1-2.

[2] F. von Hügel, *Eternal Life* (Edinburgh, 1912), p. 365.

[3] In *De Toto*, Barfield equates feeling and thinking with enjoyment and contemplation. Lewis separates the mind's "contemplation," that which it thinks true, from "enjoyment," that which one feels or inwardly experiences, hence the need for myth.

[4] Lewis, *Christian Behaviour* (London, 1943), p. 18: "A Christian society would be what we now call Leftist."

[5] In several letters to Greeves c. 1930, Lewis mentions reading Eastern religious texts and practising "mind-emptying" meditation.

[6] Probably derived from Macdonald, *Lilith*, rather than from Jung.

[7] John Betjeman, "May-day Song for North Oxford," in *Collected Poems*, 3rd ed. (London, 1970), p. 118, in allusion to an "earnest ethical search for the *Logos*."

[8] On Greek problem of One and Many, see Barfield, *Romanticism Comes of Age*, pp. 47-55.

[9] In *De Toto et Parte*, Barfield listed, but never wrote, six further definitions, viz.: VII Image: "A part realised as its whole by another part;" VIII *Time*: "The image of the sundering of part from whole;" IX *Space*: "The image of the sundering of part from part;" X *Body*: "The image in space of form;" XI Soul: "(i) The image in time of form, (ii) The image in time of spirit;" XII *Spirit*: "A part being the whole."

[10] Steiner, *Knowledge of Higher Worlds*, p. 217.

CHAPTER 7

[1] "Mental picture" (Steiner's *Vorstellung*) : a mental creation of a scene, as distinct from a copy in the memory. In *Saving the Appearances*, p. 23, Barfield extends his term "representation" to mental creation in terms of any of the five senses.

[2] Actually (as Mr Summerfield points out) the concluding sentence of Temple's essay "Of Poetry." See *Works of Sir William Temple* (London, 1814), III 443.

[3] Barfield wrote "No" in MS.

[4] Wordsworth, *The Prelude* (1850), II 315-18.

[5] Barfield, *Poetic Diction*, p. 144.

[6] ——, *Romanticism Comes of Age*, p. 84 ff.

[7] Popper, *Logic of Scientific Discovery*, pp. 40-42; also Ch. IV, *passim*.

[8] John Stuart Mill, *System of Logic* (London, 1843), II. iii. 3.

[9] In lectures delivered in 1964 at Drew University, Barfield, following Coleridge, cited Ludovico Vives for *phantasia* as an active power and imagination as passive (Drew Lecture 10A, in Wade Collection).

[10] Discussed in Barfield, *What Coleridge Thought*, p. 78.

[11] Barfield, *Romanticism Comes of Age*, pp. 28-29.

[12] Cap. vii, cited in Evelyn Underhill, *Mysticism* (London, 1911, rpt. New York, 1961), pp. 55-56.

[13] See Barfield's brilliant discussion of "Imagination" passage, in "Either-Or" essay.

CHAPTER 8

[1] Barfield, *Poetic Diction*, p. 141.

[2] Tennyson, *In Memoriam* LVI, 7 (q.v.).

[3] Cf. Plato, *Theaetetus*, 155C and Coleridge, *Aids to Reflection* (Bohn ed.) CVII (reference supplied by Dr Whalley).

[4] I. A. Richards, *The Philosophy of Rhetoric* (London, 1936), p. 96.

[5] Shakespeare, *Macbeth*, V.v.17-28.

[6] Lewis, *Summa* II, sections xix, "Imaginative art"; xx, "Symbols and Myths, what"; xxi, "The content of Myths"; xxii, "The abuse of Myths."

[7] Lewis comments approvingly of Maeterlinck in several letters to Greeves during 1916-17, calling *The Blue Bird* "a glorious book" and saying he reads many works for their "peculiar mystic dream-like atmosphere."

[8] In a "Great War" letter not placed in sequence, Lewis defines myth and legend, apparently at Barfield's request: "A *myth* is a description or story introducing supernatural personages or things, determined not...by motives arising from events within the story, but by the supposedly immutable relations of the personages or things...and not...connected with any given place or time." A legend he defines as "believed by the teller to be true, but departing from truth unconsciously...in the interests of greatness, the marvellous, or of edification."

[9] Francis Bacon, *Advancement of Learning*, II.v.3, cited in Barfield, *Poetic Diction*, p. 86, with comments from Shelley, "Defence of Poetry."

[10] Cf. I *Corinthians* ii. 13-16.

[11] Santayana, *Works, loc. cit.*; George Macdonald, *Phantastes*, Ch. XXIV.

[12] Cf. Barfield's remarks on "idolatry," in *Saving the Appearances*, p. 110f.

[13] "Myth became Fact" in W. Hooper (ed.) *God in the Dock*, pp. 63-67.

[14] In letter to Greeves, No. 124 (1 June, 1930), Lewis expresses dislike of Greek text of Fourth Gospel, and in "Modern Translations of the Bible" (1947), in *God in the Dock*, pp. 229-33, points out the un-literary quality of New Testament language.

[15] See Lewis, *Surprised by Joy*, pp. 13-14.

[16] Lewis, journal-letter to Greeves, 5 November 1929, No. 107 in Wade Collection, where Lewis says this is a "peculiarly British characteristic."

[17] George Macdonald, *At the Back of the North Wind*.

CHAPTER 9

[1] Lewis, *Miracles: A Preliminary Study* (London, 1947), p. 25: "Those who (like myself) have had a philosophical rather than a scientific education find it almost impossible to believe that the scientists really mean ... that the movements of individual units ... are in themselves random and lawless."

[2] Barfield, *What Coleridge Thought*, Ch. 3, especially pp. 34-35, and "Either-Or" essay.

[3] Term well explained in R. J. Reilly, *Romantic Religion*, p. 13 ff., which has an excellent chapter on Barfield.

4 Coleridge, *Biographia Literaria* Ch. XII, Thesis VI, Shedd III, 344-45: "it is a subject which becomes a subject by the act of constructing itself objectively to itself; but which never is an object except for itself, and only so far as by the very same act it becomes a subject."

5 Coleridge, "Theory of Life," cited in Barfield, *What Coleridge Thought*, p. 79 ff.

6 Barfield, "Either-Or" essay (1971); Blake, "Letter to Thomas Butts" (22 November 1802), line 88.

7 On this antithesis, see William James, *The Varieties of Religious Experience* (London, 1902; New York, Modern Library rpt.), pp. 407-10.

8 Known by Kant and Coleridge as "Practical Reason."

9 See Barfield, *Speaker's Meaning*, Ch. III: "The Psychology of Inspiration and Imagination."

CHAPTER 10

1 J. C. F. von Schiller, "Die Asthetische Erziehung des Menschen" (1795), *Werke* (Darmstadt, 1962), Bd. II, p. 630: "Darin also kesteht das eigentliche Kunstgehemmis des Meisters, dass er den Stoff durch die Form vertilgt." (In *De Toto*, Barfield gives the German, for which I have substituted my own translation.) Schiller argues that since all raw material is resolved into the work's form, the reader or spectator experiences only the finished product. He therefore condemns art designed to teach or to play on emotions, for beauty's total effect is freedom from passion. See his *Letters on Aesthetics*, #22.

2 Barfield, "Form in Art and Society," *The Golden Blade* (1951), 88-99, reprinted in—"*The Rediscovery of Meaning" and Other Essays* (Middletown, 1977), pp. 217-27.

3 Vladimir Soloviev, *The Meaning of Love*, trans. Jane Marshall (London, 1945).

4 Lewis, "De Descriptione Temporum" (Cambridge, 1955).

5 On Barfield's argument, "die," "death," and "hero" would all have been contained within some primal word signifying a mythic rather than historical event, e.g. the death of Baldur.

6 On subject-object dichotomy, see Barfield, essay 'Either-Or" and *Speaker's Meaning*, p. 110 ff.

7 See Barfield, *What Coleridge Thought*, pp. 45, 132-33, 257 n. 21.

8 Coleridge, *Biographia Literaria*, Ch. XIII.

CHAPTER 11

1 Mr Barfield comments in a letter that he personally could not complete *De Toto* owing to pressure of legal work, and that once converted to Christianity Lewis "lost all interest in the issue."

[2] See remarks on metaphor in Lewis, "Bluspels and Flalansferes."

[3] Lewis, "Modern Theology and Biblical Criticism," in *Christian Reflections*, pp. 152-66.

[4] Asserted in condemnation of Arnold Bennett as a "priggish hack," in letter to Greeves dated 25 October 1916 (No. 39 in Wade Collection). Mr Summerfield informs me that the work in question is Bennett, *Literary Taste: How to Form It* (London, 1909).

[5] Especially in Lewis, *Experiment in Criticism* (Cambridge, 1961).

[6] See James G. Colbert, Jr., "The Common Ground of Lewis and Barfield," in *Bulletin of New York C. S. Lewis Society*, No. 70 (August 1975), 15-18.